IMAGES OF MAN

IMAGES OF MAN

**Studies in Religion
and Anthropology
Lectures by
Distinguished Visiting Scholars
at Wake Forest University**

*Edited by
J. William Angell and E. Pendleton Banks*

Luce Program on Religion and the Social Crisis

*Carlton T. Mitchell
Series Editor*

ISBN 0-86554-124-8

All books published by Mercer University Press are produced
on acid-free paper that exceeds the minimum standards set by the
National Historical Publications and Records Commission

Library of Congress Cataloging in Publication Data

Main entry under title:
Images of man.

(Luce Program on Religion and the Social Crisis; 1)
Includes bibliographies and index.
1. Man (Theology)—Addresses, essays, lectures.   I. Angell, J. William (John William)   II. Banks, E. Pendleton.   III. Series.
BL256.I4   1984   291.2'2   84-14687
ISBN 0-86554-124-8 (alk. paper)

50, 508

CONTENTS

PREFACE

This volume is the product of an interdisciplinary seminar conducted by the Department of Religion of Wake Forest University with financial aid provided by a special grant from the Henry Luce Foundation. This generous grant made it possible to plan a series of six symposia on the general theme of "Religion and the Social Crisis." Two Wake Forest professors, J. William Angell of the Department of Religion and E. Pendleton Banks of the Department of Anthropology, have edited and contributed to this volume. It reflects the theme followed in a university course that they jointly taught during the spring of 1982 with the aid of six visiting lecturers who have also contributed to this collection.

Our request to the Henry Luce Foundation was made by members of the Department of Religion on the assumption that our society is in radical crisis because, among other reasons, the various academic disciplines have fragmented into isolated specialities. The failure of scholars to enter into dialogue across their disciplines has more than academic consequences; it also signals the loss of any integrating center of social value and religious meaning. Far worse, it marks the end of a common sense of what is peculiarly human.

The original grant proposal was not premised on the hope that a grand ideology will emerge to reunite the splintered disciplines and restore human life to its lost wholeness. But as long as some of the major academic fields—particularly religion, the social sciences, and the professional fields of law, medicine, and business—continue largely to ignore each other, enormous damage will be done both to the academy and to society. The primary aim of what came to be known as the Luce Program has been to foster both mutual understanding and criticism, in the hope that we might begin once more to ask what it means to be uniquely human and thus better to address the various social crises of our time.

The Luce Program has six distinct component parts that complement each other in the development of the general theme, "Religion and the Social Crisis." A total of more than thirty distinguished lecturers will have visited the campus by the time the enterprise is completed in 1985, and an equal number of Wake Forest professors will have participated actively in some phase of the project. In 1981, Wake Forest professors Ralph Wood of the Department of Religion and Jon Reinhardt of the Department of Politics led the first series on "Civil Religion in America." In the 1983 series, Professors John Collins of the Department of Religion and Frank Wood of the Department of Psychology explored the relationships between their two disciplines.

During the fall of 1983, Professor Carlton Mitchell directed a program on "Values in Teaching and Professional Ethics" with the assistance of Dean Thomas Mullen of Wake Forest College, Dean John Scarlett of the School of Law, Associate Dean Nat Smith of the Bowman Gray School of Medicine of Wake Forest, Dean Robert Shively of the Babcock Graduate School of Management, and Dean Thomas Taylor of the School of Business and Accountancy. Ten visiting scholars, representing all of these professions and higher education in general, worked in teams of two each week for five weeks in order to enrich this project. Also in the fall of 1983, Professor McLeod Bryan organized a symposium on the theme of "Communities of Faith and Radical Discipleship." Six visiting scholars representing several disciplines presented papers in dialogue with the well-known German theologian, Jürgen Moltmann.

The lectures in this present volume were delivered to public audiences, and open discussion followed. Students also had the opportunity to respond to the lecturers during class sessions. Other faculty members were engaged in more informal dialogue. During the spring of 1984, the final Luce program will consider the topic, "The Religious Institutions and the Social Crisis."

It is our intention to make the entire Luce lectures in "Religion and the Social Crisis" available for a wider audience by publishing four subsequent volumes as well as this initial series. The Henry Luce Foundation deserves our deepest gratitude for making this project possible through its grant. The

Luce Program has generated lively and fruitful debate on the Wake Forest University campus, and it has encouraged a continuing dialogue among the disciplines. We are especially grateful to Martha Wallace and Robert Armstrong of the Henry Luce Foundation for their encouragement. Dr. Watson E. Mills of the Mercer University Press has been of great value in this publication. Ms. Ann Francis, secretary to the Department of Religion, has been one of our most valued assistants, not only in the typing of many manuscripts, but in the general planning associated with this venture.

Carlton T. Mitchell
Series Editor

IMAGES OF MAN
IN THE
HEBREW-JEWISH-CHRISTIAN
TRADITION

J. William Angell

The underlying purpose of this series of studies is to present a variety of views concerning the nature and condition of mankind as determined by the disciplines of theology and anthropology with the hope that a contribution may be made toward understanding and solving the human crises of our time. We acknowledge, of course, that such a purpose is far too ambitious. Nevertheless, as academicians working in related fields, we must assume that it is our task and privilege to contribute all that we can to the understanding and improvement of humanity.

This essay is a revision and summary of two lectures presented to the seminar led by Professor Banks and myself and reported in this volume. If the two disciplines we represent can be as compatible and cooperative as we were, their work and service in the future will be both friendly and fruitful.

Modern Western views of man have been derived for the most part from Greco-Roman philosophical foundations and Judeo-Christian religious concepts. The ancient sources have been transmitted and reformed by the cultural forces of the Middle Ages and the Renaissance, both of which, it is important to remember, are exclusively Western designations. The various philosophical and theological anthropologies thus accumulated and passed down have been, in turn, reformulated and sometimes radically changed by the rationalism and empiricism of the Enlightenment, and especially by the work of modern archaeology, sociology, psychology, and anthropology. The result is that modern Western views of man are varied and rich, but they also frequently lack synthesis.

What are the essential elements in the images of man that have been formed by such influences in the long history of the West? Perhaps more important for the present study, what are the factors in the nature and condition of humanity that collectively contribute to the crises in human existence, and what are the resources at hand that may help to meet and overcome the crises?

I

Man in Ancient Hebrew
and Jewish Thought

The primary source available to us revealing the observations and reflections of the ancient Hebrews about the nature and condition of man is that collection of literature known to Jews as *Tenakh* and to Christians as the Old Testament. The varied materials in that sacred canon, accepted as such by later Judaism, Christianity, and Islam, were written and edited between 1000 B.C. and 150 B.C., though some of the traditions had their origins many centuries prior to their final formulation. In addition to this source, similar views of man may be found in later Jewish literature—the Apocrypha, the Pseudepigrapha, the traditions contained in the Talmuds, and the writings of Jewish scholars that were perhaps best exemplified by Philo of Alexandria (early first century).

Some of the fundamental conceptions of human nature found in that ancient Hebrew/Jewish literature may be summarized as follows:

(1) Human beings are characterized by a duality of nature. All of us are "from the dust," a part of the natural order; but we possess at the same time the power of self-transcendence, the ability to choose, to think in abstractions, to be aware of ourselves as well as others, and to exercise at least a small degree of self-determination. The Hebrews spoke of these two sides of man as *ruach* (spirit) and *basar* (flesh). Both are derived and creaturely, they believed, but spirit is that faculty of man which is God-like, whereas flesh is weak, dependent, and constantly subject to decay and destruction.

Being flesh means that man is subject to all the so-called laws of nature: limited by space and time, determined by ineluctable causation, and marked by pain, disease, and physical death. Although the ancients did not know or use the language of modern science, this view of man is compatible with more sophisticated scientific description. On the other hand, since human beings are also spirit, they are thereby capable of moral responsibility, social development, and the understanding and control of nature. Although they remain a part of nature and subject to its regularities, they at the same time possess the capacity to rise above the creation to a degree that makes them only a little lower than the Creator. According to the Hebrews, this dual condition and capacity is both the glory and the peril of man.

(2) Man is necessarily bound to community, and although individuality is desirable and needed, it is a constant danger, requiring the recognition of the priority and the greater good of community. In simplest terms, every person is the product of community—a father and a mother, each of whom is in turn the product of parents, grandparents, and extended families reaching out and back through innumerable generations. "No man is an island." This fundamental fact of human life points to the family as the basic unit of society, as the Hebrews recognized. For that reason they developed strict regulations for family organization and conduct, many of which have been built into the mores of subsequent Western culture. The abandonment of those structures and mores in contemporary society may be a primary cause for the loss of community and the presence of social crises.

The primacy of community in Hebrew consciousness and behavior provided the central context for religious expression in the idea of covenant. The concept of covenant has been traced far back in the history of the Near East. It was a common instrument of social organization among the Hittites and other ethnic groups of early antiquity, and the Hebrews adopted the idea not only in the structures of their society but also as the symbolic means by which they were related to Yahweh, their particular God. Those Hebrews who entered into a binding and demanding covenant with Yahweh thus became a holy and separate people—Israel, the People of God.

Many significant results flowed from this creative concept of community. One was an emphasis upon morality understood as obedience to the commandments of God as the father/husband, the lover and sustainer of his people. Another was the unusual perception by Israel of the tentative and fragile relation to its God. Its covenant with Yahweh was an artificial relationship, not a natural one. The blessings of life that the people enjoyed, and even life itself, were dependent upon the graciousness of Yahweh, and unfaithfulness to him meant the breaking of the covenant, with the resultant dissolution of the community. A third consequence of the central fact of covenant in Israel was the centripetal power of community as opposed to the centrifugal danger of alienation. An individual has no reality or value outside the community of family, people, and faith; but within the com-

munity each member has protection, direction, and even the hope of immortality through the continuing generations.

(3) Human beings are subject to the transitoriness of history and are
destined for death, but they may also find courage in a vision of purpose
and deliverance through a relationship to permanence. The Hebrew/Jewish
understanding of man in this way contributed a unique theme to Western
thought, one that has continued to appear in various manifestations. Prominent among them are the assumption that history is linear, moving toward a
predestined goal, and the unusual belief in a final restoration of all persons
for judgment and for timeless fellowship with the deity or for permanent
alienation.

The genre of apocalypticism was the chief means by which Judaism and
Christianity developed and expressed these ideas. They have become the
commonplaces of Western culture. The language is bizarre, highly imagi-
native, and often beyond rationality. Nevertheless, the visions have provided
hope in times of despair, and the dreams have become the substance of faith
to lighten a frequently dark and empty future.

(4) Human beings are capable of transcending themselves and the rest
of nature in spite of their creatureliness and boundness, precisely because
they have been endowed with spirit, a likeness to the infinite and eternal
Creator. The awesomeness and mystery of the whole natural order bear witness to a source of power, wisdom, and goodness, a witness evident to the
open mind and the eye of faith. However, because creaturely selves are inevitably self-centered, choosing idols for worship, the Eternal Creator makes
himself and his will known also in certain chosen events and persons of
history.

The Hebrews expressed this conviction about mankind by speaking of
sin, revelation, and faith. They believed that all human beings are alienated
from the Creator, Yahweh, the Covenant God of Israel, and therefore are cut
off from light, life, and goodness. But because God is everlastingly gracious, provision is made for forgiveness, restoration, and renewal. Thus the
very likeness to God that human beings possess as God's greatest gift is
both the source of their alienation and the ground of their reconstitution.
God does not destroy or coerce the freedom that he has given mankind;
rather, he constantly attempts to renew the power of freedom by winning
mankind's affection and faithfulness.

(5) Human beings are morally responsible. Their capacity for knowledge and freedom enables them to know and choose the true and the good,

or to refuse them. However, they must then continue to live under the conditions of their choice. Moral responsibility has two meanings, then: on the one hand, it designates the ability to respond, to say yes or no, to answer when called; on the other, it indicates the burden of accountability, that whatever is sown will be reaped.

One of the remarkable features of the earliest-known Hebrew religion was its insistence upon the inseparability of religion and morality. That was not true of most ancient religions, with their human sacrifices, disregard of basic human value and rights, corruptions of priestcraft, exploitation of children and women, the poor and the outcast. In the Hebrew traditions God was the advocate of Abel, the slain brother of Cain, and God forbad the ritual sacrifice of the first-born, Isaac, by his father, Abraham. The prophets of Israel, beginning with Samuel's rejection of Saul and Nathan's rebuke of David, did not cease to condemn the mighty because of their injustices and to call all the people to the practice of righteousness. The legacy of Israel demonstrates that religion is empty without ethics, that no faith is worthwhile without the fruits of righteousness and justice.

These five primary assumptions concerning the nature and status of man, along with others that might be listed, are the composite anthropology of the Hebrew/Jewish tradition that has been part of the very foundation of Western civilization. The ideas were carried on in Christian teaching, in which they were combined later with many elements of Hellenistic thought; and they have remained formative factors in our theoretical and practical heritage.

II
Man in Early Christian Thought

Christianity arose within Judaism. Jesus himself, the founder and center of the new way, was a loyal Jew of the land of Israel. He and his immediate followers accepted the major elements in the faith of their forefathers, including the principles listed above. These elements were especially compatible with the interpretations represented in their time by the Pharisees, the Essenes, and the apocalyptists. The teachings of the Hebrew prophets were the bedrock upon which most of the teachings of Christianity were constructed. Thus the new faith was marked more by continuity and reform than by discontinuity and innovation.

Nevertheless, it would be wrong to deny that there were and are different emphases and additional teachings in the new way espoused by Jesus and the Apostles. They did not reject the religion of their past and their people, but they did continue the prophetic criticism of some of the practices in Judaism. Moreover, they specifically claimed that the God of the Covenant was doing a new thing—as he had promised he would—especially in and through Jesus for the redemption not only of the people of Israel but for all mankind.

This truth may be understood as the basis of the new elements of anthropology that have remained at the heart of Christian teaching. At least four of these elements should be recognized.

(1) According to the Christian faith, the initiative of God in the life of Jesus of Nazareth is the sine qua non of any hope for mankind, nature, and history. This is the essential meaning of the doctrine of incarnation. Jesus was not just another man, even the wisest and best of men. He was the Creator within the creation, born, led, and empowered by the Spirit from beyond the creation, coming out of the grace of the Creator to renew the corrupted creation, especially mankind, by recapitulation and reconciliation.

This fundamental affirmation received a variety of expressions in the traditions of the early Christian communities, many of them still extant in the collection of writings known as the New Testament. There are recorded the stories of the spiritual conception by Mary, a virgin of Nazareth. There are also the claims by Jesus and about Jesus: that he was the promised Messiah, the King of the Kingdom of God, the High Priest in the heavenly sanctuary, the apocalyptic Son of Man, the Lord of all nations, the Lamb of God, the final Judge of history.

All of these grand titles and symbols suggest relevant meanings for the Christian teachings concerning the nature and destiny of mankind. However, none of them is more significant for our purposes than Paul's characteristic claim that Jesus Christ was and is a second Adam, the firstborn of a new spiritual race, born of the very creative Spirit of God. By identification with him all people may find new life and well-being. The claim that the eternal has appeared in time, specifically in Jesus (which is the doctrine of incarnation made most explicit in the Gospel of John), is further explicated by Paul in his teaching that Jesus is the new mankind in whom all may experience a new creation.

(2) A second new element in Christian teaching relevant to man is concerned with the hope of resurrection. This idea was not originated by Christians, for it had been debated and proposed earlier in Judaism and in other

religions. However, in Christianity the claim is made that Jesus has already been raised from the dead, a foretaste and guarantee of the future possibility for believers at the end of history. And, in what is the new aspect of the teaching, Christians taught that the bodily resurrection of the believer in the eschaton will be grounded in the power of God's grace rather than in a natural capacity of immortal man.

The distinction between resurrection and immortality is crucial, though frequently overlooked. Generally, the Greeks sought after and believed in the natural immortality of the human soul. Plato, for example, taught that the soul, the spiritual essence of the person, is immortal and possessed of innate truth and virtue. The tragic condition of the soul is due to its association with unstable temporality and matter: "The body is the tomb of the soul." This condition may be rectified by the vision, love, and practice of virtue. In addition, the Hellenistic mystery religions provided myths and rituals intended to aid the soul in its search for enlightenment and purification.

On the other hand, the ancient Hebrews apparently viewed mankind as a unitary being, the soul (*nephesh*) being the total self. Not only that, but all human beings are bound together in a common humanity that, in turn, has chosen alienation from God and is therefore in the condition of death. If there is hope, mankind must first be restored in community, in a covenant. Each person may or may not participate in that restoration by being related to the covenant people. If the individual is to survive an inevitable physical death, it may be in terms of the continuation of the community of which he is a part, or it may possibly be in terms of an eschatological restoration of the individual by the resurrection of the body, the whole person. Thus immortality is a gracious gift to those who were dead, not an inalienable condition of the soul. The earliest Christians, notably the Apostle Paul, followed that view of resurrection, which was still being debated and formed in Judaism. However, Paul and the other Christians claimed that their belief in the eschatological resurrection of mankind was grounded in their historical experience of the risen Jesus, rather than in theological reflection and apocalyptic hope alone.

(3) A third new element in the Christian view of man may be seen in the proclamation that God has renewed the broken covenant of Sinai in the death of Jesus Christ, thus forming a new Israel. Just as there is a second Adam in Christ, there is a second Israel in the Church. The *Qahal* has become the *ekklesia*. But whereas the old People of God were descended from Abraham according to the flesh, now the new People of God are the children

of Abraham, in the sense that he was the father of all the faithful, without distinction between Jew, Greek, or barbarian. There is no longer distinction between male and female, slave or freeman, between the circumcised and the uncircumcised. All people are invited and urged to participate in the new status and condition of mankind through repentance and faithfulness.

(4) Another new element that Christian teaching added to its Jewish heritage concerning mankind is the change in the view of morality. The Law and the Prophets had called for righteousness and justice as obedience to the command of God, especially as the fulfillment of the obligations inherent to the covenant with Yahweh. There was the implied assumption that the people of Israel could "do justice, love mercy, and walk humbly with God" if they would only choose to do so. The major stream of Christian teachers, beginning in apostolic times, emphasized the prior necessity of a new relationship of faith to God, from which, as "the fruit of the Spirit," righteousness would grow like good fruit on a good tree. The difference is not absolute and should not be pressed too far. However, the subtle change in emphasis is noteworthy and has been significant in the subsequent history of moral teaching.

III
Man in the Christian Tradition

Christian anthropology has been developed as an aspect of theological reflection throughout the history of Christianity. The biblical principles, sketched above, have remained the primary ingredients, but the development has been complex and varied as new ideas have been added and new influences have been brought to bear on the original teachings. Here we will take note of only a few of those new ideas and influences that have contributed to the modern Christian understanding of the nature and condition of man.

Although no dogma of man has been agreed upon or promulgated by any authoritative body in Christendom, the classic understanding that has received the most widespread acceptance grew out of the Augustinian/Pelagian debates of the early fifth century. Pelagius was a British monk who went to Rome around A.D. 400. He and his followers, especially Celestius and Julian, later bishop of Eclanum, defended the full divinity of Christ against the Arians and the full humanity of Christ against the Manichaeans. In the exposition of the latter orthodox view, they insisted on the essential goodness of the creation, including mankind. Apparently also motivated by a strong desire to reform the lax morality of many Christians, they taught that the human will is morally free to choose the good and to refuse the evil, and that the grace of God is available to all as a "help" in exercising that freedom. Specifically, Pelagius rejected St. Jerome's radical asceticism, which resulted from the assumption that the flesh is corrupted by sin. He also challenged the famous prayer of St. Augustine in his *Confessions*, "Give what thou commandest and command what thou wilt."

The ensuing controversy resulted in the Augustinian doctrines of man, sin, and grace. In a modified form these doctrines became the standard teachings of the Church, especially in the West, during the Middle Ages. Indeed, the Reformers, especially Calvin, generally accepted the Augustinian view, and a similar emphasis has reappeared in the twentieth-century theology of Karl Barth, Reinhold Niebuhr, and their colleagues.

Against the Pelagians, St. Augustine argued that mankind has lost the original innocence and goodness it was endowed with by the Creator. By the misuse of freedom, man has chosen sin and death, thus losing his freedom. He is henceforth bound by his choice. However, the grace of God is given in Christ and made available through the Church, so that life and virtue may be restored. Logically, according to St. Augustine, this prevenient grace, including even saving faith itself, is the gift of God and is given only to those of God's own choosing. This doctrine of double predestination thus intends to give all the glory to God by insisting that God's justice is preserved in the condemnation of the wicked while, at the same time, God's mercy is manifested in the redemption of the elect.

In his frequently repeated formula, St. Augustine taught that, in his original state, man was free not to sin and not to die (*posse non peccare, posse non mori*). But the observable fact is that mankind has chosen to sin and thus to die (*non posse non peccare, non posse non mori*), and continues to exist in that tragic condition. The gift of God's grace, however, can make possible a new condition for mankind so that he is no longer disposed toward sin and is given immortality (*non posse peccare, non posse mori*).

These views of the nature and condition of mankind, which dominated Western culture for a millennium, have been challenged and frequently rejected by the elements of modernity that arose out of the Renaissance and especially the Enlightenment. The study of classical humanism gave rise to a primary concern with man rather than God, this world rather than any other possible world. Reason became the ultimate authority for truth and right rather than Scripture, Church, or dogma. The scientific method has become the accepted means for the understanding and control of nature, including humanity. Discovery and exploration have opened undreamed-of frontiers, both on the earth and beyond, so that mankind has simultaneously grown smaller in the cosmos and greater in power and possibility. The philosophy of progress has become an assumed article of faith for modern man, and that assumption has borne fruit not only in theories of evolution concerning the development of nature, including human beings, but also in theories of history, economics, politics, religion, and morality.

However, because of a series of tragic calamities in the twentieth century, beginning with the sea change set in motion by the First World War and continuing into the present nuclear crisis, a radical reappraisal of the condition and capacities of mankind appears to be in order. The "Age of Anxiety" has dawned. The awesome problems are everywhere apparent, at every level of human life, but solutions are few and mostly inadequate. The question is no longer what the future of mankind will be like, but whether there will be a future at all. The ancient apocalyptic visions may become a frightful reality.

IV

Sources of Hope

The purpose of this study is to survey some selected images of man that are available in our crisis-ridden world today. The subject is approached from the perspectives of anthropology and religion, two disciplines that are related, at least by a common concern with the nature and destiny of mankind. Anthropology is the historical and empirical study of people. Religion pursues precisely the same interest. Perhaps the two can continue to join forces for the understanding of ourselves and our needs so as to provide experience, knowledge, and possibly also hope, in the midst of the present crises.

BIBLIOGRAPHY

Augustine. *City of God*. Garden City: Image Books; Doubleday and Company, 1958.

————. *Confessions*. Garden City: Image Books; Doubleday and Company, 1960.

Barth, Karl. *Church Dogmatics*. Volume 3, part 2. Edinburgh: T. and T. Clark, 1960.

Brunner, Emil. *Man In Revolt*. Philadelphia: Westminster Press, 1947.

Calvin, John. *Institutes of the Christian Religion*. Philadelphia: Presbyterian Board of Christian Education, 1936.

Kierkegaard, Søren. *The Sickness Unto Death*. Princeton: Princeton University Press, 1946.

Luther, Martin. *The Bondage of the Will*. Grand Rapids: Baker Book House, 1976.

Niebuhr, Reinhold. *Moral Man and Immoral Society*. New York: Charles Scribner's Sons, 1932.

————. *The Nature and Destiny of Man*. Two volumes. New York: Charles Scribner's Sons, 1943.

Robinson, H. Wheeler. *The Christian Doctrine of Man*. Edinburgh: T. and T. Clark, 1911.

Tillich, Paul. *Systematic Theology*. Volumes 2 and 3. Chicago: University of Chicago Press, 1957, 1963.

ORDER AND DISORDER
IN THE
HOUSE OF ISLAM

Robert F. Spencer

I

The drama began about A.D. 610 in the cave on Mt. Hirā near the settlement of Makkah, a stopping place on the Arabian caravan route to Palestine. The archangel Gabriel, the Prophet Muhammad's visitant, brought the beginnings of the divine message:

> Proclaim aloud!
> In the name of your Lord
> Who created
> Who created Mankind
> From a clot.
> Proclaim!
> For your Lord is most Bountiful,
> He who teaches with the Pen
> Teaches Mankind what they know not . . .
> (Sūrah 96:1-5)

Unleashed, the drama of Islam became a force in the medieval world, suffered a period of stagnation, and gives the appearance today of regaining its vitality.

What indeed is Islam? A religion, to be sure, however difficult to define the term may be. But it is much more. It is a congeries of institutions that are interrelated, a major civilization that makes an indelible imprint on world history, a cultural and social system that past and present touches intimately the lives of its millions of adherents. The religious pattern has served to integrate, to weld states and communities, and to provide that set of premises and postulates about the human condition and its relations to the divine in which all Muslims share. In the broadest sense, Islam is a distinctive culture.

There is in Islam no equivocation: God is. It cannot be said that "God exists," since such an utterance implies that there are phenomena independent of God; nothing has being except God. The human being, created by God from dust or at birth from a clot, has no alternative but an Islam, a "submission" to the divine will. By recognizing their own dependence, persons become Muslims.

The message imparted to the Prophet Muhammad, the proclamation of the word of God, emerges as the Qur'ān—the recitation—a blueprint not only for the human perception of the divine, but for social structure, societal organization, and their associated legal foundations as well. The Qur'ān is the source, the fountainhead of human knowledge. From it the Muslim learns his place in the divine plan and from it too he is provided with a model for action, in terms of both private and public behavior (cf. Bell, 1963).

It is tempting here to dwell on both the sources of Muhammad's message and to move at once into the deeper theological implications of the Qur'ān, considering its form and style, its compelling linguistic beauty. The Muslim views it as God's word. The question is, does God utter his word at a point in time, thus creating his utterances for mankind, or conversely, does the Qur'ān coexist with God from all eternity? The question preoccupied the medieval theologians; much ink and much blood were spilled over the issue. It may be asked if in this there is a touch of Hellenism, a *logos*, an "In the beginning was the word . . . ," as Christian tradition has it. To admit that something can exist outside of God, even his word, is *shirk*, a sin of polytheism. Such scholastic matters aside, it is apparent that Islam has undergone innumerable trials in the course of its emergence from a desert revitalization movement to its present status as a major world religion.

Whatever its sources, Jewish, Christian, Hellenistic, Zoroastrian, it developed its own distinctive set of traditions and its autonomy. Although its prophetic character (taking as its prophets Adam, Noah, Abraham, Moses, Solomon, Jesus, and Muhammad himself) may be aligned with that of the Near Eastern religious triad, and although it shares with its Christian and Jewish counterparts an inflexible monotheism buttressed by a sacred text, it still stands apart. Being unique in its own view and convinced of its own rectitude, Islam has never made common cause with the systems whose traditions it partly shares.

The differences in Islam lie not so much in theology—Muslim unitarianism could make perfectly good sense in some Western circles—as they do in the design for living that the Qur'ān and its commentaries present. A social mode arose with the religion, one essentially incompatible with either Western or Jewish background and ideology. It is the social system rather than the pattern of belief that gives Islam its particular ethos and flavor.

A word must therefore be said about the nature of this ordered society. If it is one integrated through religion, as is the case both historically and to a degree even now, it follows that there is a precise body of traditions making up the Muslim complex. Although the formulation so often voiced in cultural anthropology of the "great" against the "little" tradition may have some relevance here, it is basically that the former implies history, the latter a synchronic appraisal. In anthropology, despite a once well defined orientation to the historical (whether of actually documented history or a historical "reconstruction" in the mode of Boas and Kroeber), contemporary attention in the discipline appears to focus on the essential synchrony of human phenomena. The result is that when attention is paid to the local community, the village, or as now, the city, these are not seen as end points in a historic process but rather as describable entities in which the element of time is all but ignored (cf. Eickelman, 1981:ch. 3; Eisenstadt, 1973). This point can be made especially in regard to the Muslim world and the Middle East, where the element of time has always played so significant a role (Haddad, 1981). Islam has tended to a literalism not unlike that of the Christian fundamentalist and creationist. To a Muslim, the justification and rationale for the divinely ordained social order clearly lies in the historic reality of Muhammad and his companions.

The historic tradition and social system are spread from north and west Africa through the Middle East to the subcontinent and Indonesia. Regardless of sectarian differences, there are sets of unifying symbols, institutions, and behavior patterns that characterize Muslims wherever they may appear. The theologians have taken cognizance of these, so much so as to evolve from the Qur'ān and the *hadīth*, the practices and sayings of the Prophet attributed to members of his entourage of Makkan converts, a series of religious and social "pillars" on which the socioreligious complex rests. Because these are often misunderstood in the non-Muslim world, it is worth noting them and considering their import. Indeed, it is from them that a meaningful perspective on Islam can be derived. They involve not only theology and philosophy, but social structure and legal aspects are in some measure subsumed as well. Contained herein are duties and obligations incumbent on all believers.

As is well known, Islam is a religion without a clergy. True, there are men—and some women today—who, learned in the Qur'ān and the law, assume positions, however informally, of recognized religious leadership. Still, they occupy a place basically no different from that of any devout believer. Thus each person is in effect his own priest; he recognizes a sacerdotal duty to the first two pillars, *shahhadah* and *salā*. The first is testimony, a witnessing, the second is prayer and the postures and attitudes associated with it. To repeat *"Ashshadu anna lā ilāha ila' llāh, wa Muhammad rasūlu' llāh"* is to put Islam, so to speak, in a nutshell. "I testify that there is no God but God and Muhammad is God's *rasūl*" (ambassador, representative, Gesandter, etc.). Familiar enough words, yet a primary affirmation of faith, of a concept wholly fundamental in Islam.

Faith is thus primary and requires affirmation. On the Day of Judgment, when the hosts of humanity will appear before the mercy seat of God, there will be those condemned to hell-fire because of actions forbidden by God. One does not refer to "sins"; a world burdened by sin and guilt plays considerably less a role than in the Christian context. God condemns principally because the individual denies him. Unbelief (*kufr*) is the cardinal transgression. The believer is rewarded with paradise. Hence to articulate the *shahhadah* is to affirm the requirement of faith.

The second pillar relates to the first. This is *salā*, prayer. Tradition developed the conventional five prayers per day, beginning at dawn and carrying through into the darkness of the night. Such prayer is not a petition, a request to God for the fulfillment of some unsatisfied need. On the contrary, because he is totally omniscient and almighty, God will provide as he sees fit. Nor can the feeble importunings of humanity cause him in any way to alter his divine plan. Prayer is thus glorification: *"Allāhu akbar!"* "God is the greatest!" Prayers may vary from such exclamations to recitation of various of the sūrahs of the Qur'ān; all such utterances serve only to extol the powers and majesty of God. Yet God is merciful and reads the hearts of humans, judging intention. He will provide if his plan is in accord with human wishes, but "Give us this day our daily bread . . ." has no Muslim role.

It is on the level of witnessing and prayer that overt religious behavior appears. True, the five prayers may be private, but the duty of each believer to perform them is clear. Here too are the various attitudes of prayer, the personal ritual of posture and obeisance. Although not in themselves Quranic, these are forms so widely diffused through the Muslim world as to be recognizably a vital element in religious behavior.

Testimony and prayer are not without their social implications. Even though prayer is largely a private matter, there is the assemblage in Muslim communities for the noon prayer on Friday. The community itself is a body of judgment on the basis of demonstrated piety; through various cues the devout are recognized. It is this conformity to religion that acts as a stabilizing influence in the local community, whether in a village, a nomadic encampment, or in a town or city quarter. By the same token, traditional communities assemble lists of devout men, such as could lead the Friday prayer, or act as witnesses in a court case. These are married men, fathers of children, of whose religious commitment there is no doubt. Such men are known to pray and to engage in the personal ritual of glorifying God.

It is in regard to the third pillar that the Muslim sense of societal obligation arises. Muhammad laid stress on the concept of *'ummah*, a community of the like-minded faithful. The indigent, the widow and orphan, were seen as charges of the community and it was to their benefit that the *zakah*, the alms tax, was instituted. To offer a full appraisal of the social implications of this levy, one must examine the social organization of Makkah and the Hijāz as it was at the time of the Prophet (Gaudefroy-Desmombynes, 1950:32, passim; Hodgson, 1974: 1:181). As Islam became urbanized, this element took on the aspect of an income tax, usually computed at two and a half percent. The *zakah* was arithmetically formulated in the Qur'ān and may be seen as a reflection of the marked concern, both there and among the Arabs generally, with property and material goods. There is emphasized, moreover, the concept of social roles, the responsibility of mankind for mankind within the Muslim context.

The economic concern is worth stressing. Alms-giving relates to this, but so do many other aspects put forth by the Qur'ān that touch human life as it must be lived in the community. This emphasis is so marked that it is perhaps no accident that the punishment for theft is stringent or that usury is so vehemently forbidden. Quite apart from the demands of *zakah*, the support of one's less fortunate fellows, much attention is given to the question of inheritance of property by female as well as male heirs. True, a woman inherits half of what her brother may take from a patrimony, but she has rights to property, including ownership of her own bridal wealth.

Since so much of the Qur'ān concerns itself with economic matters, the religiocultural system appears to stress a this-worldly quality and orientation. In sum, there is little room for mysticism. That mystics did arise, appearing within a century or two after the death of the Prophet, might indicate a dissatisfaction with the eminently practical and nonspeculative quality of Islam itself. With the various Sūfī movements there is a parallel to the gnosticism of early Christianity. Clearly, both Hellenistic Gnosticism and Buddhism play a part in the Sūfī development. Nonetheless, such a mystic and other-worldly quality is not contained in the gospel of Muhammad, which reflects a quite down-to-earth practicality. This fact is pointedly apparent in the *zakah* complex.

The point of commemoration is to be found in the two final pillars. *Sawm*, fasting, applies to the ninth lunar month, while Ramadan is the rule that nothing should pass the lips between dawn and dark. Commemorated is the time when the Qur'ān "came down" to Muhammad through the archangel. Although today few Muslims know the basis for the month-long fast, it is an institution that is rather rigorously observed. When the Tunisian premier, Bourguiba, tried to get the jurists in Cairo to excuse his civil servants from the fast on the ground that their efficiency was sharply reduced, his plea fell on deaf ears. The Cairene legists might have issued a *fatwa*, a legal opinion that, although not binding, might still have justified the action. The fast also has its social component. The pious Muslim who observes the fast, who avoids not only food and drink, but also tobacco during the sacred month in the daylight hours, affirms his status as devout.

Finally, there is *hajj*, pilgrimage. Every Muslim avidly seeks to make the pilgrimage to Makkah and the other holy places at least once in the course of his earthly sojourn. If unable to do so, he may pay a professional pilgrim to do it for him. He will have the clothes in which he will be buried, and in which too he will appear before God on the Last Day, dipped into the well of Zamzam. The well is associated with Ishma'el, son of Abraham by Hagar, since it was into this desert that the jealous Sara'i drove her husband's concubine and her son. The intervention of the angel and the flow of the miraculous spring saved the lives of Hagar and Ishma'el, the latter living to become the founder of the Arab tribes. Thus the pilgrimage honors not Muhammad, even though he lived in Makkah, but rather Abraham. He is seen as an earlier prophet, one who enjoyed a close communion with God and came near to sacrificing his son. Blood sacrifice is still performed in association with the pilgrimage. The returned pilgrim, from Africa to Indonesia, is honored in his home community; his presence accords status both to him and those of his extended group. However much the religion of Islam has fallen on evil days, the symbol of the pilgrimage serves to reinforce the traditional.

The five pillars bring to the fore the two chief elements in the religion of Islam. There is first an *ᶜibādat*, servitude, the recognition of one's dependence on God and one's duties to God. Second, there is a *muᶜamallah*, an obligation to humanity, or paralleling the Christian context, to one's neighbor. It is the latter that gives Islam its specialized ethos, one possessing political as well as social and economic aspects. Muhammad's significant contribution, which became tribalism in the Hijāz and Makkah, was the creation of the *'ummah*—the community of believers bound together in common belief and behavior. The ensuing tradition creates ideally an egalitarian society and community with defined sets of social and legal norms. In this, all persons stand equally before the judgment seat of God.

Tradition, insufficiently rooted with the death of the Prophet in 632 A.D., was given a direction that Muhammad himself clearly could not anticipate. A notion of *primus inter pares* arose with the problem of his succession. A strict Islam admits no leadership: kings and sultans, wazīrs and wālīs, shahs and emperors technically have no place in the democratic theocracy that Muhammad instituted. The rationale for this is in a concept of regency and delegation of powers. A primary purpose of political authority rested in the juridical organization, the fact that leadership was conceptualized as an implementation of canonical laws. The community was, and is, localized. But in the Muslim concept, certainly after the Prophet's death, it went beyond locality and became worldwide, extending as far as the proselytizing religion could reach. A developing tradition, after 632 A.D., had it that the Prophet's mantle should pass to a successor selected by a consensus (*'ijmāᶜ*) of believers. This did take place, so that Abū Bakr, ᶜUmar, ᶜUthmān, and ᶜAlī followed in order. These were the Makkan, the "rightly guided" caliphs, the *Khalīfah*, "successors" who were members of the Prophet's family and members of his entourage. Nonetheless, the problem of political dissension was quick to arise.

At this point there appears on the scene what has incorrectly been called the basis for Muslim sectarianism. Numerous schismatic groups came into being early in the development of the system, a concomitant perhaps of the growing pains associated with the shift from erstwhile tribalism to the urbanization associated with the rise of the ᶜUmmayyads in Damascus. The division between Sunnah and Shī'ah, itself a reflection of the question of political succession, is not primarily a religious one. The history is interesting and complex, but it may suffice to note that Sunnah has admitted the consensual element based on the Qur'ān and the actions and sayings of Muhammad; Shī'ah held more strictly to a notion of succession based on the family of the Prophet, the descendants of ᶜAlī married to Fātimah, the daughter of the founder. The more populous branch, Sunnite Islam, kept alive the caliphal concept, the successorship of the Prophet, which created a unity of the larger part of the Muslim world. The institution of the caliphate lasted until 1924, when it was abolished by the decree of Kemâl Atatürk in Turkey. Shi'ite Islam, on the other hand, tending more toward the mystical, chose to stress the idea of martyrdom and suffering and created a millennial idea to the effect that a messianic *'imām*, a community head, would appear. Yet despite these differences, Sunnite and Shi'ite Islam are not fundamentally diverse. Points of issue between them are said to constitute a "family quarrel" (Hodgson, 1974, passim).

This is not to say that Islam was without its sectarian differences. However much the community ideal may have permeated Muslim thought throughout history, interpretations varied and one viewpoint replaced another. Mention is made of the medieval argument of the created versus the uncreated Qur'ān, while such issues as rationalism and free will often stood sharply against predestinarianism. Similarly, a number of movements, both social and religious, came into being at various times. But these need occasion only minimal delay; they occur within a context of a set of beliefs and essentially fixed concepts, themselves variations on a constant theme of divine majesty and human subservience to it. To be sure, they range from the strict literalism of the modern Wahhābis to the Neo-Platonism of the Spanish Muslims in the Middle Ages or of al-Ghazzālī (d. 1111) and his Sūfī successors. Yet together all such viewpoints are congruent with the overarching and distinctive civilizational pattern of an Islam.

Even if one can discern the character of the community and the social and institutional elements resident in it, attention must still be paid to the theological implications of Islam. It may be understood that despite the impact of events, whether in the medieval political and military conflicts or in the rise of nationalist ideologies today, the Muslim theistic quality has its own distinctiveness, certainly as compared with the perception of the divine in either Christian or Jewish circles.

The point is made that God is eternal, omniscient, compassionate, possessing a host of qualities defined so explicitly in the Qur'ān. Man's helplessness and predetermined course aside, there is still the prevailing notion of a human will. This is both problematical and paradoxical. Islam admits no concept of sanctification; there is no "leap into faith" in Kierkegaard's terms, nor yet any sense of a faith effected by the gift of the Holy Spirit. The relationship Man-God is at base simplistic. God created Man (from the dust of the ground) to echo his own praise. God then asks the angels to acknowledge the supremacy of the human creation. All agree except 'Iblīs (Satan), whose arrant pride banishes him from God's presence. It is he, the "slinking whisperer," who constantly seeks to undermine what God has achieved. God, meanwhile, is anthropomorphized. Reference is made to his throne, his hand, his arms, his head. He presides in Paradise and has ordained the Day of Judgment, the end of the cycle of creation.

Clearly, man can neither understand what God is nor attain any awareness of his motives. If sectarianism exists in Islam, it is often on the basis that knowledge of God and his will can be derived from careful and intuitive reading of the Qur'ān, or conversely, that questions had best not be asked and will be answered on the Last Day. One cannot, in short, question God or probe his actions. He is unknowable and inscrutable, giving man only the crumbs, so to speak, from his table. His is transcendent and yet immanent. He reposes in celestial majesty and yet he is "closer than the jugular vein" (Sūrah L:16). It is precisely this implicit paradox that has preoccupied Muslim theologians through time.

A solution to the problem of knowing God's qualities has led, in Sunnite Islam, at least, to nominalism. God is known by his epithets, by the "most excellent Names" that describe his aspects. These are largely adjectival, reflecting Arabic lexeme building, and essentially Quranic. God has ninety-nine names; a hundredth, like that of the Old Testament YHWH, is hidden. God is Creator, Sustainer, Ruler, Destroyer, Restorer, Recorder, the Exalter, the Honorer, and certainly the Compassionater and Compassionating (McDonald, 1961:35). To know the names of God, to recount them on the rosary, is to bring the divine closer to the human. But this is hardly theology.

Nominalism represents a conventional approach to God. To the Muslim, rather than involving himself in speculative theology, it is generally regarded as sufficient to affirm one's Islam and thus to find the basis of commitment in the sense of Muslim community identity. It may, of course, be agreed that there is theological refinement at various times and among Muslim scholars through the ages. There is, for example, the issue posed by the Muᶜtazilites, the rationalists, who saw in the epithets given above a contradiction of the concept of divine oneness (Fazlur Rahman, 1979:61-63). Or conversely, there were the predestinarians, the Qadarites, who, like the Wahhābi of today, place all in God's hands (Smith, 1959:48-51). In the end, despite dialectic, or the intuitive knowledge implicit in the relationship between God and mankind, the ontological propositions of Islam hark back to an idea of the "good." For the community it is not the issue of faith or nonfaith that is primary—such faith is assumed and expected—it is rather that divinely instituted patterns of behavior set the Muslim off from the unbeliever. "I am a Muslim" implies far more than voluntary acceptance; through Islam there is an awareness of an ordered universe.

To this point the concern has been with a historic tradition, the civilization of Islam, one to which the devotee is committed through history and which to him appears wholly ordered and fundamental. Mention is made, by way of example, of the economic concerns apparent in the Qur'ān. But to this may be added a series of such legalistic matters as family structure, the Arab notion of familism in Quranic guise, marriage, parenthood, inheritance, and certainly, divorce. The Qur'ān is wholly precise in every regard. It defines with exactness the roles of men and women, "and men are a degree above them" (Sūrah 2:228), implying that conventionally women have half the value of a male. This point emerges both in regard to the allocation of property and in witnessing a legal case. Women inherit half of what a male relative may expect; similarly, the legal testimony of two women is worth that of one male.

Just how specific the Quranic legal regulations are may be illustrated in the matter of marriage and divorce. Marriage is an expected state; indeed, the definition of adulthood requires that the individual be married and a parent. This is a reflection of the Arab tribal stress on genealogy and descent. A man, of course, may have four wives, however much monogamy was and is a general practice. Marriage is secular, a contractual arrangement between groups of kindred, often with a preference for a patrilateral parallel cousin union. Equally traditional is the right of the male to divorce, giving rise to the pattern of divorce by formula, a pronouncement uttered three times after successive menstrual periods (Spencer and Busool, 1982). The legists, using various and often labored and devious arguments based on Quranic exegesis, differ as to the role of the witness in such procedure. Or, to phrase the matter differently, the Qur'ān does not provide an answer to all human questions. Hence there is the *Sunnah*, the orthodoxy of interpretation, the *hadīth*, the narrative chains, consensus, analogic reasoning, and *ijtihād*, systematic reasoned judgment. All of these apply not so much to religion as they do to a legalistic tradition (cf. Cragg, 1965, 1969). In divorce, once it has taken place and the bride wealth is paid in full, the ex-husband has the right to take her back in marriage again and may do so freely. The process may be repeated. A third remarriage, however, is not possible unless the woman in question marries another and is widowed or divorced from this second husband. She is then legally free to return to her original husband. Whatever the explanation for this complexity—and opinions differ—this is only one of the legal issues so spelled out in Muslim culture.

II

Every culture, as Spengler notes, actualizes its prime symbol. In the case of Islam, this clearly is God. Spengler argues that this is true even though the rise of the religion came too late to allow the kind of impact on the world that, for example, resulted from the appearance of Hellenized Christianity. Whether there is agreement with Spengler or not, he appears to recognize how it is that the Arab-Muslim sphere comes to be different and to possess its own distinctive character. His formulation of the "Magian Soul" is different from the "Faustian" ethos of Western scientific man.

On this level, of course, one is confronted with the "great tradition," the historical force and role of Islam through the ages. But this is so abstract as to be scarcely satisfying. However much one may give thought to a world of Pan-Islam, to see the institutions of the Qur'ān reflecting a historic trend of traditionalism shared by all Muslims, the issue of a world divided rather than unified under the aegis of religion is probably more relevant than an abstract historical overview.

The point is well made by Geertz when, as an anthropologist, he compares a perception, based on his own field endeavors, of Morocco and Indonesia (Geertz, 1968). Both are Muslim lands, but there is a world of difference between them. Thus there are more reduced traditional modes, those limited in time and space, reflecting local custom and history. In the Islamic world this has always been true. It may be that the Iranians resisted the encroachment of Arab Islam and the imposition of the Arab language by choosing association with their own brand of Shī'ah. Such examples of local interest, those stemming so frequently from pre-Islamic patterns, suggest not vast differences of opinion or sectarian developments, but rather the kind of phenomenon one encounters in Christian Europe. Spain and Italy are Roman Catholic countries, but there are striking differences between Spanish and Italian Catholicism, or between Irish and Polish. Local customs and interests across so wide a geographic area as that encompassed by Islam cannot be ignored.

To a degree this localized focus stands against the ordered system and its religious foundations. Historic events have also militated against unity. When the Mongols sacked Baghdad in 1250 A.D., or when the caliphate passed from the Arab ᶜAbbāsid house to the Ottoman sultans, the foundations of the Islamic world began to rock. Cultural vitality among the Arabs—inventiveness, art, science, and literature—that was apparent in the Middle East and in Spain began to erode; the torch was passed to the West, to Italy of the Renaissance and to Europe at large. The Muslim states were left in a position of marginality and a long and stagnant career followed. True, the basic premises of Muslim religious, social, and intellectual life remained, but in essence the spark was gone. There arose a period of what Watt has called "the sclerosis of . . . theology" (Watt, 1962:149).

In the twentieth century the pendulum has begun to swing again. It is by no means easy to assess what appears to be a contemporary renascence. This is because the ordering of the religious society has been subjected to influences for which Muhammad and his followers made no provision. The modern world has introduced patterns and elements with which Islam was ill-prepared to cope. The goal of many is a united Islam, not necessarily under the caliphate as it was, but with the sense of community that early Islam so passionately upheld. A difficulty is that no agreement can be reached on what kind of Muslim world should come into being.

The varying impact of the West on Islamic states today has to be considered. Technological supremacy and imperialism in Western terms made a stagnant Islam subservient. In addition, the Muslim states were obliged to cope with new intellectual streams. Capitalism stands against Marxism, and since World Wars I and II, the rise of nationalism and the repudiation of colonial status has made for a divisive course. Can the Muslim retain his religious dedication and live a life according to the Quranic model; or, by accepting various Western notions, does he part company with religion and abandon his religious devotion? Is there, for example, a burden of national guilt when Pakistan builds an atomic reactor, when the Egyptians make common cause not so much with Israel as with the West at large, or when the nations making up OPEC set a new price for oil?

The point is that Islam has been obliged to come to grips with the demands of the West and does so not as a religion, but rather as a series of national units, all preoccupied with local self-interest. This is difficult and often accompanied with severe growing pains. The result is a spectrum that ranges from a sharply defined literalist fundamentalism to shades of liberal humanism (Arberry, 1968; Eisenstadt, 1973:25). Western Europe and the United States, although they may still fight this battle, have been generally able to put it effectively aside, largely, one may suppose, because religion in the West does not serve as the primary element of societal integration as it has done so extensively in Islam.

One thinks at once of the essentially reactionary regimes in Iran, Libya, or Pakistan. Does, for example, the questionable government of the Ayatollah Khomeini really seek to turn the clock back to the early middle ages and so to revive a society as it was in Makkah and Madīnah in the days of the four "rightly guided" caliphs? Aside from the political aspects, it is apparent that so-called fundamentalist movements are appearing sporadically in the Muslim world. These are unquestionably responses to what is seen as the unholy influence of the West with its alcohol, blatant sexuality, and secularized modes. More than this pietistic and antisecular orientation, however, there is a response in the Muslim world to what is seen as Western imperialism both politically in the past and economically in the present. The various Arab nations have been able to make effective use of oil even though not all the states share equally in this natural resource. Given the economic preoccupations of the Qur'ān, it is perhaps not surprising that an ideology of wealth should penetrate Muslim consciousness, or even that in the literalism and extreme pietism of Saudi Arabia with its Wahhābī philosophy, there is no rejection of materialism.

Viewing political and economic issues as effects rather than as causes, one must note such effects within a context of cultural orientations. Islam is shaped by its history, to be sure, by the events and accidents of time. Whether nationalist interests prevail, whether the various forms of Marxist ideology are accepted or rejected, whether a Saudi businessman buys a hotel chain in Belgium or land in Florida, neither the sense of God's immanent presence nor the concept of the community and its laws are lost. The point is that Islam is immensely practical and pragmatic; God may be transcendent, his ways inscrutable, yet he has created a real world. It is this general acceptance of objective reality that operates in the Muslim sphere. Heaven can wait; meanwhile, there are the real problems of living in God's world according to his law.

There are exceptions, naturally. On a folk level, one cannot rule out local sets of symbols and customs. Or, because Islam possesses so earthy a quality, there are those religionists who find in Sufism and in parallel gnostic orientations the awe and thrill, perhaps otherwise lacking, that some scholars have long regarded as integral to a definition of religion (the "mood," the pantheistic viewpoint, as some see it [LaBarre, 1970:329]). The godlessness of Marxism-Leninism may be repugnant, even if there are many today who see in the various shades of socialism and communism the fulfillment of the ideal of divinely instituted community. Whatever the direction of modernization in Muslim lands, it seems clear that there are new tasks assumed by the contracting and expanding elements inherited from the great civilization of Islam.

At this point one should move more specifically into the local and national scene so as to consider the contemporary role of the religion of Islam. How far, for example, does the traditional legal system continue to apply? Many Muslim states have banned polygyny by law. In Turkey, Egypt, and a number of other areas women have been allowed to stand for a place in the national parliament and, as advocates and judges, to assume roles in the legal structure. But this is a departure from tradition. Similarly, divorce by formula has become rarer. In various localities one may increasingly see ostensibly devout women wearing the veil and the garments, such as the Iranian *chadur*, which hide the limbs and so deter depravity. These and other examples of a "return to religion" require assessment in terms of individual and group motivation.

With the return to religion in response to various distracting features of modern times, there is an understandable search for the fundamentalist pillars of Islam. A world gone astray, turning its face from God, is to be rejected, allowing the divine laws to enter again, and recreating through God an awareness of the "good." The problem, as it currently exists, arises from the paradox of the acceptance of Western technology and at the same time, of a renewed search for traditional values. Obviously, the resolution cannot be realized. For this reason, so thoughtful a scholar as Fadlur Rahman notes that there is an essential failure to retain an adequate traditional base and fundamentalism today has only local meaning (Fadlur Rahman, 1981:23-35). There are "layers" of tradition, the major tradition of Islam, it is true, but there are also the cross-currents of interest and aspiration that only serve to create confusion among the Muslims of today.

For example, how does the corner grocer in a poor quarter of Damascus respond? Any moderate success or failure in his business hinges on the will of God. Living as he does in the neighborhood of a city, he meets the demands of the surrounding community: he prays, he attends the mosque on Friday at noon, he offers credit but accepts no interest (though is not above accepting a gift), he marries off his daughters, and sees that his sons attend a mosque school in addition to the secular education provided by the state. One cannot probe his beliefs too deeply and can only recognize that he shares in the major tradition of Islam. Misfortune is *Mā shallah*, "what God has wished," and an enterprise is accompanied by the phrase *In shallah*, "if God so wishes." He listens to his radio, or if lucky, watches his television, and marvels at the continuing manifestations of the will of God. Comparatively, the peasant making a bare living from farm production is not in a very different situation. On the other hand, the intellectual élites flirt with new ideologies or, resisting the baleful influence from the West, and like the Muslim jurist-theologians of the Middle Ages, swing back to the dictates of religious tradition.

It is not to be implied that the present Muslim scene is wholly intellectually stagnant or medieval in concept and tone. The West—perhaps still harking back to the Crusades or, as one writer puts it, considering Islam with much the same horrified shock that greeted 1917 Bolshevism—has long stereotyped Islam as fanatical and unyielding. Assuredly there are these elements, and Iran and Libya may provide cases in point: however, segments of Christianity display these elements also. Islam has its own "moral majority," its rigid fundamentalists in the Western sense, those who vigorously oppose the teaching of biological evolution in secular schools. Planned parenthood, abortion, the prohibition of alcohol—familiar enough topics in the West—evoke much the same positive and negative responses in Muslim circles. The liberal and devout Muslim tries for something else beyond managing these issues. Without involving himself in political ideology, he seeks to make Islam one with a changing world.

The thoughtful Muslim is obliged to recognize that Westernization and all that it implies—urbanization, industrialization, and secularization—are here to stay. The answer for the future lies not in the total repudiation of the

West as the Imām Khomeini would have it, nor in the kind of aggrandized Muslim imperialism of Qadhāfi. The late Anwar Sadat had a future vision, as did the Shah of Iran. Yet neither of these was able to decide on a rationale for the course of the faith. Perhaps it necessarily comes back to Sir Muhammad Iqbal, an Indian Muslim who died in 1938. His idealism held that God himself awaits the fulfillment of human genius and potential (Iqbal, 1962; Schimmel, 1963). Muslim unity is not yet, but God may eventually ordain it.

There is justification for asking whether a modern Islam can achieve any intellectual competition with the West or whether it must forever remain bound to its traditional mode. Clearly, not so long as Quranic literalism is present and negativism, shrouded in the hatred directed to the state of Israel, becomes a rallying point. On the other hand, there are the moderns and near-moderns who have attempted to break the ties of the past, not so much in departing from what the religion holds as basic truths, as in finding new ways of interpreting. One thinks of Iqbal, or of Muhammad ᶜAbduh in Egypt, humanists and poets with a vision of Man, State, and God in harmony. An answer, one most pointedly reflective of current directions, is a variation on an old theme, a time-honored juridical idea in Islam. This is the concept of *ijtihad*, which is a reasoned judgment and generally involves an analogic means of interpretation. While much dependent on the primacy of the Qur'ān, the concept allows expansion. However much the Muslim thinker may choose to reject the philosophical systems of the West, its systems should be examined, accepted, rejected, all in accord with the unfolding plan of God. It is this trend that may allow the world of Islam to come more adequately to grips with problems of today.

REFERENCES

Abdelkader, Z.

    1973 "The Reactivation of Tradition in a Post-Traditional Society." *Daedalus* (American Academy of Arts and Sciences) 102:225-37.

Abdullah, Y.

    1938 *The Meaning of the Glorious Qur'ān*. Text, translation, and commentary. Two volumes. Cairo: Dar al-Kitāb al-Misri.

Ali, Shariati.

    1974 *Islamic View of Man*. Houston: Islamic Literatures, Inc.

Arberry, A. J., ed.

    1968 *Religion in the Middle East: Concord and Conflict*. Two volumes. Cambridge: Cambridge University Press.

Bell, R.

    1963 *Introduction to the Qur'ān*. Edinburgh: Edinburgh University Press.

Cragg, K.

    1965 *Counsels in Contemporary Islam.*. (Islamic Surveys 3). Edinburgh: Edinburgh University Press.

    1969 *The House of Islam*. Belmont CA: Dickenson Publishing Co. (The Religious Life of Man Series.)

Eickelman, D. F.

    1981 *The Middle East: An Anthropological Approach*. New York: Prentice-Hall.

Eisenstadt, S. N.

    1973 "Post-Traditional Societies and the Continuity and Reconstruction of Tradition." *Daedalus* (American Academy of Arts and Sciences) 102:1-28.

Fazlur, R.

    1979 *Islam*. Second, revised edition. Chicago: University of Chicago Press.

    1981 "Roots of Islamic Neo-Fundamentalism." In P. H. Stoddard, D. C. Cuthell, and M. W. Sullivan, eds., *Change and the Muslim World*, 23-35. Syracuse: Syracuse University Press.

Gaudefroy-Desmombynes, M.

    1950 *Muslim Institutions*. London: Allen and Unwin.

Geertz, C.

    1968 *Islam Observed: Religious Development in Morocco and Indonesia*.

New Haven: Yale University Press.

Goldziher, I.
  1925 *Vorlesungen über den Islam*. Heidelberg.

Haddad, Y. Y.
  1981 *Contemporary Islam and the Challenge of History*. Albany: State University of New York Press.

Hodgson, M. S.
  1974 *The Venture of Islam*. Three volumes. Chicago: University of Chicago Press.

Iqbal, Sir M.
  1962 *The Reconstruction of Religious Thought in Islam*. Lahore: M. Ashraf Publisher.

LaBarre, W.
  1970 *The Ghost Dance: Origins of Religion*. New York: Doubleday.

Levy, R.
  1962 *The Social Structure of Islam*. Cambridge: Cambridge University Press.

McDonald, D. B.
  1961 "Allah." In *Encyclopedia of Islam*, 33-42. The Hague: Mouton.

Nader, A. N.
  1956 *Le Système philosophique des Muᶜtazila*. Beirut.

Schimmel, A. M.
  1963 *Gabriel's Wing: A Study into the Religious Ideas of Sir Muhammad Iqbal*. (Studies in the History of Religions) Leiden: E. J. Brill.

  1975 *Mystical Dimensions of Islam*. Chapel Hill: University of North Carolina Press.

Smith, W. C.
  1959 *Islam in Modern History*. New York: Mentor Books.

Spencer, R. F. and A. Busool
  1984 "Divorce, Remarriage, and Tradition in Muslim Society."

Stieglecker, H.
  1959 *Die Glaubenlehren des Islam*. Munich.

Stoddard, P. H., D. C. Cuthell, and M. W. Sullivan, eds.
  1981 *Change and the Muslim World*. Syracuse: Syracuse University Press.

Watt, W. M.
  1962 *Islamic Philosophy and Theology*. (Islamic Surveys 1). Edinburgh: University Press.

Images of Man, Nature,
and the Supernatural
in the Buddhist
Schema of Salvation

Melford E. Spiro

I have been asked to address the theme, "Images of Man, Nature, and the Supernatural" from the perspective of Buddhism. Since the subject is vast and a paper requires a focus, I shall be concerned with these images in relationship to the Buddhist conception of salvation, for I take it that is what any of the world religions is ultimately about.*

Buddhism originated in India in the sixth century B.C., and soon spread throughout Asia. With the exception of Malaya, Indonesia, and the Philippines, as well as India, its original home, Buddhism to this day continues to be the dominant religion of Asia.

Like all of the world religions, Buddhism very early split into various groupings, based on important doctrinal differences. The two major contemporary groups are geographically separated. One, known as *Mahāyāna* ("The Great Vehicle"), is found in North and East Asia, especially in China, Korea, Japan, Tibet, and Mongolia. The other, known as *Theravāda* ("The Teachings of the Elders")—the Mahāyānists refer to it by the pejorative, *Hinayāna* ("The Lesser Vehicle")—is found in South and Southeast Asia, most especially in Sri Lanka, Burma, Thailand, Laos, and Cambodia.

It is Theravāda Buddhism that I shall examine in this paper, not only because I have observed it firsthand—intensively in Burma, and casually in Sri Lanka and Thailand—but because the composite images of man, nature, and the supernatural that are reflected in its doctrines and inform its

*I wish to acknowledge the helpful suggestions of David K. Jordan, Marc J. Swartz, and Donald F. Luzin.

conception of salvation are probably unique in the history and anthropology of religion. For that reason these images provide a dramatic contrast with the images projected in the other religions that are addressed in this volume. Thus although the doctrines of Mahāyāna Buddhism would most certainly be characterized as false by Western religionists, they would nevertheless most likely concede that Mahāyāna is still a religion. On the other hand, in addition to characterizing the doctrines of Theravāda as false, they would also almost certainly deny that it is a religion.

Theravāda Buddhism—hereafter referred to simply as "Buddhism"— is based on a materialistic metaphysic that denies the existence of a soul or self. Indeed, the doctrine of no-soul or nonself (*anattā*) is one of the three essential doctrines of Buddhism. According to this doctrine, human beings, like all sentient creatures, are composed of five material aggregates or *khandhā*—literally, "heaps"—that at death disintegrate without residue. These "heaps" consist of matter (the body), feelings, perceptions, impulses, and consciousness. The belief that there is a self, a soul, or an "I" that inhabits the body, coordinates its actions, or survives its death is for Buddhism an illusion.

Buddhism goes even further than this. In its thoroughgoing materialism, it denies the existence not only of a soul or self, but also of a God, if that term means—as it means in Christianity and Judaism—a supernatural Creator and Savior. There are, to be sure, numerous supernatural beings in Buddhism, some of whom have relationships with the human world. But the Buddhist gods are far removed from the Western conception of the supernatural. First, none of the gods created the world, none sustains or directs it, and none guides its destiny. Second, like humans, the gods too are mortal. Although they live in various celestial abodes, the gods originated as ordinary mortals who, by virtue of their *karma*—a term to which I shall return—were reborn in their present form, which is transient. Hence they, like all other sentient beings, will eventually be reborn into any number of other forms and planes of existence until or unless they finally attain *nirvana* (another term I shall examine below). Third, although some of the gods may assist human beings to deal with problems of their mundane existence, none can help them to transcend or overcome that existence, or to attain the supreme religious goal of salvation. In short, none of the gods is a Redeemer or Savior; since they themselves are in need of redemption, they can hardly assist others to attain that goal.

But what about the Buddha? Isn't he God? Although, unlike the Judeo-Christian God, he is not a Creator, is he not a Redeemer? Is it not redemption that they seek from him when worshiping at a pagoda or in a temple, Buddhists make their obeisance before his image? The answer to these questions is an unqualified "no." The Buddha is not a god because, having attained salvation (nirvana), he is infinitely superior to any god. Nevertheless, he cannot save others because having attained salvation, paradoxically enough, he no longer exists—not, at least, in any ordinary meaning of "existence." Before I examine the paradox of a salvation religion without a Savior, it is perhaps desirable to add a few additional comments about this man who founded the religion that bears his name.

"Buddha," like "Christ," is not a proper noun, but a title. A Buddha is, literally, a "Supremely Enlightened" person, one who has not only attained salvation—that is a goal many persons have attained—but who has discovered the Path to salvation, and moreover, has taught that Path to others so that all mankind might be saved. However, since the knowledge of that Path is periodically lost in each world cycle—of which there are many, extending over eons of time—numerous Buddhas arise, each of whom teaches an identical message.

The present Buddha was born as an Indian prince, Siddhartha Gautama, in the sixth century B.C. Reared within palace walls amidst the luxuries of the royal court, Siddhartha was entirely devoted to the pursuit of worldly pleasure. Then, unexpectedly and successively, he encountered the three forms of misery that are the lot of all human beings, commoners and royalty alike; that is, he encountered a sick man, an old man, and a corpse. Overwhelmed when informed that he and all other human beings were subject to the same miseries of illness, old age, and death, he renounced the world—his wife, his children, the throne, everything—and retired to the forest in order to find the Path of deliverance from these miseries. Having discovered that Path after six years of searching, he nevertheless delayed his own deliverance so that he might share his discovery with others. Upon his death—forty-five years later—he immediately attained nirvana, which means that unlike gods and men, insects and cattle, he is no longer alive.

But if the Buddha is not alive, to whom and for what does the Buddhist pray when he worships the Buddha? Strictly speaking, he does not pray to or for anything because in the Buddhist context, "worship" is best glossed as "to give homage," "to honor," and the like. To worship the Buddha is to pay him homage for having discovered the Path, which if followed can lead to salvation. Hence in the words of the liturgical formula, the worshiper "take[s] refuge" in the Buddha, the first of the three Buddhist "gems," just as he "take[s] refuge" in the two other "gems": the teachings of the Buddha (*Dhamma*) and the monastic order (*Sangha*) that he founded.

The absence of any true supernatural beings in Buddhism is a corollary of yet another of its central doctrines, that of impermanence (*anicca*). Since, according to the latter doctrine, everything in the world, from atoms to empires, is in a perpetual state of creation and dissolution, there can be no supreme reality that transcends the universal condition of endless flux.

The doctrine of impermanence has important implications not only for Buddhist theology—its image of the supernatural—but also for its anthropology—its image of man. Thus the doctrine that man has no permanent self or soul is obviously a corollary of the doctrine of impermanence, as is the doctrine, not yet discussed, that suffering is one of mankind's salient characteristics. The latter doctrine requires extended discussion because it is central to the Buddhist conception of salvation and hence its image of man's highest aspiration.

The central message of all the world religions, we might say with Max Weber, is their soteriological message, their message of salvation or redemption. If each of these religions has a different soteriological message, however, it is because each has a different perception of the human condition, of the characteristic of man that necessitates redemption. If man is viewed—as he is viewed in Christianity, for example—as existing in a state of sin, then redemption consists of deliverance from sin. Although Buddhism too views man as a sinner, it views sin not as inherent, but rather as a contingent characteristic of the human condition, a characteristic that can be overcome. For Buddhism it is suffering that is the inherent characteristic of the human condition: therefore, redemption consists of deliverance from suffering. It was his encounter with the miseries of illness, old age, and death, it will be recalled, that led the Prince Siddhartha on his quest for Enlightenment; and that quest led to his discovery of the four Noble Truths of suffering: these concern its inevitability, its cause, its cessation, and the Path that leads to deliverance from its power.

In short, Buddhism holds no truck with that religious image of man found, for example, in certain forms of ascetic Christianity and Hinduism, and in Shiite Islam—that holds that suffering is itself a redemptive act. For Buddhism, on the contrary, suffering has no value whatsoever: it does not ennoble man, it does not build character, it does not bring him closer to genuine spirituality; above all, it is not a means to redemption. In the words of the *Sutta*, "Suffering and Release from suffering"—that is the message of the Buddha.

That life entails suffering, and that therefore all human beings suffer, is in itself a trite proposition. If, to take but one example, suffering is caused by the frustration of desire, then surely there never has been a human being who at one time or another has not suffered. The Buddhist doctrine of suffering, however, is not trite because rather than making the banal claim that all human beings suffer, it makes the radical claim that suffering is an *inherent* characteristic of human beings, and indeed of all sentient beings, including the gods.

Suffering is inherent to the human condition because, according to Buddhism, suffering is a consequence not only of the frustration of desire, but of desire (*tanhā*) itself, its gratification no less than its frustration. This radical—or, we might say, counterintuitive—claim is based on the Buddhist analysis of the relationship between suffering and impermanence. Since nothing is permanent, we attain an object of desire only later to lose it—which leads to suffering—or we worry about the possibility of losing it—which also leads to suffering. Moreover, since mental states, like everything else, are impermanent, we are never content with what we have. Having attained one object of desire, it eventually begins to pall, and since that too is a form of suffering, we either seek other objects to satisfy that desire, or we seek to satisfy still other desires. In fact, not only may the attempt to attain those objects and to gratify those desires cause suffering, but their attainment—for all of the above reasons—only leads to still more suffering.

In sum, it is the impermanence of all things, both material and mental, that accounts for the Buddhist claim that desire—the "craving" for what we do not have, and the "clinging" (or attachment) to what we do have—is the cause of that perpetual restlessness and discontent that is known as suffering. Inasmuch, then, as desire is an inherent trait of human nature, suffering—*emotional* suffering—is an inescapable characteristic of the human condition. This does not take into account the *physical* suffering that is entailed by the inescapable life-cycle crises of illness, old age, and death. Ultimately, these too, as we shall see, are also caused by desire.

Given this radical view of the cause of suffering, Buddhism holds no truck with those two secular gospels of redemption of the contemporary world: the Gospel of Social Revolution, which contends that deliverance from suffering can be achieved by the creation of a new society, one in which all desires are gratified; and the Gospel of Psychotherapy, which contends that deliverance from suffering can be achieved by the creation of a new mankind, one whose level of desire is adjusted to their capacity for achievement. From the Buddhist point of view, neither of these secular gospels can deliver us from suffering. This is not only because they cannot liberate us from illness, old age, and death, but because in their attempts to eliminate the frustration of desire neither of them attends to the root cause of suffering—the existence of desire itself.

For the same reason Buddhism does not support those religious gospels of redemption that acknowledge deliverance from suffering cannot be achieved in this world, but maintain it can be gained in the next world in some form of celestial bliss. The Buddhist rejection of the gospels of otherworldly redemption is based on the claim that desire is a characteristic of all sentient beings, from insects to gods. Since desire is its cause, there is no escape from suffering on any plane of existence, whether terrestrial or celestial. To be sure, the inhabitants of the heavens—in Buddhism there are multiple heavens, just as there are multiple hells—enjoy much more pleasure than the inhabitants of the earth. However, the belief that they have achieved deliverance from suffering is yet another illusion—like the illusion of a self or of permanence—from which they must be liberated.

In short, all of these gospels of redemption, secular and religious alike, fail because their solutions to the problem of suffering are less radical than the Buddhist analysis of the problem requires. If desire is the cause of suffering, then release from suffering can only be achieved by release from desire. Precisely that is the solution proposed by the third Noble Truth of suffering. The most prominent example of this truth is found in the paradigmatic case of the Prince Vessantara, whose life is widely celebrated, in art and drama, in the Theravāda societies of Southeast Asia.

When requested by a Brahmin to give him his beloved children, Vessantara, a previous incarnation of the Buddha, acceded to his request. Beaten and oppressed by the cruel Brahmin, the children escaped and came crying to their father, who seeing their condition, was filled with "dire grief." His heart, we are told, "grew hot within him . . . from his mouth he sent forth hot pantings; tears like drops of blood fell from his eyes." Despite his misery, however, Vessantara did not receive his children because, with a sudden and penetrating insight, he arrived at a great illumination. "All this pain," he realized, "comes from affection, and no other cause; I must quiet this affection, and be calm." Strengthened by the power of that insight, Vessantara, so the account continues, "did away with that keen pang of sorrow, and sat still as usual."

Similarly, when yet another Brahmin requested that he give him his beloved wife—who had accompanied Vessantara when he had abandoned the palace to seek Enlightenment, and gathered food for him in the jungle so that he might be able to devote himself entirely to meditation—Vessantara complied with the latter's request in the same manner. Having become "indifferent, unattached, with no clinging of mind," he parted with her having no greater regret than he would have if she were a "purse filled with coins." (The full account of the Vessantara tale, from which these quotations are taken, is found in Cowell's 1957 edition of the *Jātaka*, no. 547).

As illustrated above, the extinction of desire is the Buddhist solution to the problem of suffering. Setting aside the fact that one might question the morality of a doctrine that celebrates personal liberation at the expense of the suffering of others, that solution is somewhat surprising since it is hardly as radical as I have purported it to be, nor is it unusually profound at that. On the premise that desire creates the problem of suffering, it follows as a simple tautology that the extinction of desire is its solution. Profound or not, this solution is surprising for two other reasons as well. First, since this solution merely consists in the achievement of a state of mind—the absence of desire—it suggests that salvation must be achieved during one's lifetime. Moreover, since the extinction of desire is obviously beyond the grasp of most persons—which of us, for example, is capable of emulating the example of Vessantara?—it also suggests that the Buddhist scheme of salvation, like the Calvinist, is confined to a small band of elect.

In fact, none of these propositions is true because the third Noble Truth is not primarily a psychological truth—though it is that too—but an ontological one. To wit, since desire is a characteristic of sentient existence, the extinction of desire and hence of suffering requires, according to the third Noble Truth, the extinction of existence itself.

If this is so, then Buddhist salvation—although it is something that most of us would perhaps not view as very desirable—would now seem to be extraordinarily easy to attain. Anyone can achieve salvation simply by dying; and if one's natural death is not soon enough, one can resort to suicide in order to hasten it.

Although such a retort seems sensible from a Western and secular point of view, from the Buddhist point of view death does not bring deliverance from suffering. First, suicide most certainly does not achieve that goal because in Buddhism the taking of life, one's own no less than another's, is the most heinous of all acts. Hence rather than delivering one from the miseries of life on earth, suicide only leads to the greater miseries of life in hell. Neither does natural death bring deliverance from suffering. While death marks the end of one's life, it does not, according to the Buddhist image of nature—biological nature—mark the end of one's existence. One's present life, according to the Buddhist image of nature, is but one link in a great chain of being that comprises myriad past lives and myriad future lives, each following upon the other in relentless succession. Therefore, as death brings to an end the miseries of this life, it simultaneously ushers in the miseries of succeeding lives.

In sum, it is only when the Buddhist doctrine of suffering is placed in the context of its image of nature that it can be seen as the radical doctrine that I have been insisting it is. For given that context, when Buddhism proclaims in the first Noble Truth that life is suffering, it is stating that rebirth in any form of life, and on all planes of existence—there are thirty-one—entails suffering. When, therefore, the second Noble Truth proclaims that desire is the cause of suffering, that is because desire, as we shall see, is the cause of rebirth. Hence when the third Noble Truth proclaims that deliverance from suffering requires the extinction of desire, it is indicating that escape from suffering can only be achieved by release from the entire realm of rebirth (*samsāra*).

Clearly, then, the Buddhist solution to the problem of suffering is no less radical than its formulation of the problem. Whereas for Christianity the ultimate condition of suffering consists of eternal death, for Buddhism it consists of eternal life in what might be called the serial immortality of rebirth. In Christianity salvation consists of victory over death by the achievement of immortality in heaven or paradise, but in Buddhism it consists of deliverance from life itself, in any sense in which we normally use that term. In other words, it consists of deliverance not only from life on earth or in hell, and not only from life as a human being or as an animal, but from life in any realm, including the heavens, and in any form, including that of the gods. It is that deliverance—deliverance from the Wheel of Rebirth—that Buddhism calls nirvana, and it is the attainment of nirvana that is both the *raison d'être* of Buddhism and the only goal it views as ultimately worth pursuing.

Thus far all scholars are in agreement. Whether nirvana means the extinction of existence, or whether, less radically, it means the extinction of life as we conceive of it, is a question that prompts considerable disagreement. Reputable scholars such as La Vallée Poussin and Oldenberg claim the former to be the case, while equally reputable scholars such as Suzuki and Rahula opt for the latter alternative. Suzuki, for example, claims that nirvana refers to the extinction not of existence, but rather of the ego and its desires; and with this extinction something continues to exist, viz., "universal love or sympathy (*karuna*) for all beings" (Suzuki, 1963:50-51). Since, however, that love and sympathy are connected neither with a perceiving self (the illusion of a self has now been overcome) nor with a feeling body (the body has now been destroyed), there is no agent that experiences them. One might indeed wonder whether by this definition of "existence" there is much difference between the extinction of life and the extinction of existence. In this connection one might invoke William James's dictum that a difference must *make* a difference in order to *be* a difference.

At any rate, the kind of existence that Suzuki attributes to nirvana is probably not the kind that Western scholars have in mind when they object to the suggestion that Buddhist salvation does—or could—consist of the extinction of existence. Not surprisingly, Western interpreters of Buddhism have recoiled from that suggestion from the very beginnings of the Western encounter with Buddhism. One nineteenth-century French scholar argued that since the Buddhist people, though "not exactly like us, are, after all, our own brothers," to hold that salvation consists of the extinction of existence is not only "to malign the good sense of the Buddhist peoples," but it is also "to do injury to all humanity" (Welbon, 1967:77). "I cannot admit," cried another nineteenth-century French savant, "that three hundred million people live in the hope of their future annihilation and know no other religion than this" (Ibid:82).

In fact, as we shall see, these savants are both right and wrong. While many—perhaps most—Buddhists *believe* that nirvana consists in annihilation, they do not *hope* for their own annihilation. That, at least, is what I found to be the case in Burma, a center of Theravāda Buddhism. One informant, a Rangoon merchant, put it this way: "In nirvana there is no body, no soul, nothing (*bahma mashibu*). Who wants that?" Again, after characterizing nirvana as nothingness (*bahma mashibu*), a villager in Upper Burma expressed his perplexity concerning the wish for such a goal: "To desire nothingness is hard to understand. It is difficult, very difficult, to accept." Hence although the villager, like the merchant, believes that nirvana means annihilation, he does not wish to attain it. Rather, like the merchant—and like the great majority of other Burmans—it is his wish to remain on the Wheel of Rebirth and to be reborn as a wealthy human being.

I shall return to this discrepancy between their belief and their hope at the end. Here it is sufficient to observe that their belief is entirely consistent with the core Buddhist doctrines that I have examined thus far. For whatever the other equivocations concerning its meaning, nirvana unequivocally means that the Wheel of Rebirth has come to a halt, and that means the total destruction of the five material aggregates (*khandhās*) comprising sentient existence. Since there is no soul or self—no psychological or spiritual essence—that survives the destruction of these physical conditions of existence, it is hard to imagine how nirvana can mean anything but the extinction of existence or, as the Burmese say, *bahma mashibu*, "nothingness."

Given that the experts disagree about what is extinguished with the attainment of nirvana—whether it is life as we know it, or whether it is existence as such—it would be rash for a nonexpert like myself to attempt to resolve this issue. For our present purpose it is enough to observe that whatever their disagreement, all the experts agree that nirvana consists of liberation from the Wheel of Rebirth. If my Burmese informants, like the French savants, found it hard to understand how anyone might desire to be annihilated, in the light of our previous discussion it is even harder to understand how liberation from the Wheel of Rebirth might be achieved. For if, according to the Buddhist image of nature, birth follows death as inexorably as death follows birth, Buddhist salvation, like Christian salvation, would seem not a natural but a supernatural event, one that requires a supernatural savior. Yet as I emphasized above, there is no savior in Buddhism: the gods, who themselves have not been saved, do not have the power to save others; and the Buddha, precisely because he has been saved, cannot do so because he no longer exists. While on the one hand the Buddha exhorted his followers to "work out your salvation with diligence!" (*Dialogues of the Buddha*, 2:173), on the other hand, he admonished them that in working it out they must "look not for refuge to anyone besides yourself" (Ibid:108).

In sum, Buddhism not only proposes a radical conception of salvation, it also proposes the equally radical notion that in order to be saved man must, as it were, save himself. In order to understand how such a seemingly impossible task is possible, I will refer to yet another Buddhist doctrine, the key doctrine of karma (*kamma*). This doctrine, which is the point of intersection between the Buddhist image of man and its image of nature, explains both the process of rebirth as well as the process by which the Wheel of Rebirth can be brought to a stop.

Karma is any volitional act. When such an act is motivated by desire, then—depending on whether it is consistent with the Buddhist moral code—it creates merit or demerit for the actor. According to the Buddhist image of nature, the moral no less than the physical world is governed by natural law; consequently, karmic action no less than physical action is subject to an impersonal law of cause and effect. The karmic law of cause and effect, the law of retribution, states that meritorious and demeritorious actions, respectively, produce different effects: the former produce pleasurable consequences for the actor; the latter, painful ones. The merit or demerit created by many karmic actions, however, is of a magnitude that retribution cannot be fully worked out in one lifetime. That being the case, for each such action the retributional imbalance requires an additional rebirth—sometimes more than one—so that full retribution might be achieved. As long as action is motivated by desire, many such imbalances are created in each lifetime, and the Wheel of Rebirth continues to revolve, sometimes resting on one plane of existence, sometimes on another. In short, rebirth is caused by unfulfilled or incomplete retribution for karmic actions performed in previous rebirths.

Since retribution is only required for actions that are instigated by desire—for only they create merit or demerit—the Wheel of Rebirth can be brought to a halt by replacing desire with desirelessness, attachment with detachment (*upekkha*). Each action performed in a state of emotional detachment creates neither merit nor demerit, produces no karmic consequences—hence no need for retribution—and in the absence of unfulfilled retribution there is no cause for rebirth.

But if the Wheel of Rebirth—and the suffering that accompanies it—can only be brought to a halt by replacing desire with detachment, one might wonder how such an emotional transformation can ever be achieved since desire, according to Buddhism, is an inherent characteristic of all sentient beings. Nevertheless, such a transformation can take place, according to the fourth Noble Truth, by following the Buddhist Path, a path that consists of three successive stages: morality, meditation, and wisdom. Even to enter the Path, however, let alone to move through its successive stages, is incredibly difficult, which is why it takes myriad rebirths to achieve nirvana.

The attainment of the first stage of the Path, that of morality (*sila*), is extraordinarily difficult because to attain that stage it is not sufficient merely to follow the Buddhist moral code—the five precepts enjoining abstention from killing, stealing, illicit sex, lying, and the consuming of intoxicants. Even that is difficult enough since the telling of one lie, for example, or the killing of an insect means that the stage of morality has not been attained. But even assuming meticulous compliance with the moral code, the stage of morality has still not been attained because in Buddhism the moral life is defined not only by behavior, but also—and most especially—by intention. It is not enough to shun evil actions; one must also shun evil thoughts. Hence the attainment of the stage of morality is marked not only by abstention from stealing, killing, and illicit sex, but also by the extinction of their underlying affects—greed, hatred, and lust.

Assuming that over the course of many rebirths these immoral affects are extinguished and the stage of morality attained, this comprises only the first stage of the Path: the moral life is not a sufficient condition for salvation. To be sure, the extinction of such immoral affects as greed, hatred, and lust shortens the links in the causal chain leading from demerit to retribution to rebirth; but insofar as the moral affects—love, compassion, mercy, and the like—persist, they add additional links to the chain leading from merit to retribution to rebirth. Nevertheless, the moral life is a necessary condition for salvation because the extinction of the immoral affects results in those attributes of mind and character that are required to proceed to the second stage of the Path, the stage of meditation (*bhāvanā*).

I cannot enter here into a description of Buddhist meditation. For our present purposes it is enough to say that it is a process in which, by a minute analysis of one's own experience, one achieves existential insight into the three characteristics of sentient existence—nonself, impermanence and suffering. Without meditation these aspects, if they are known at all, are known only intellectually. Full knowledge of those three truths, however, requires not only that they be comprehended and mediated by reason, but that they be apprehended and confirmed in immediate experience. It is that kind of knowledge, the kind that can only be achieved in the crucible of meditation, that Buddhism refers to as "insight" (*vipassanā*); and it is insight into the truths of nonself, impermanence, and suffering that marks the attainment of the final stage of the Path, that of wisdom (*paññā*).

Wisdom is the last stage because its attainment leads, finally, to that goal for which the entire Path is a means, viz., the severing of all attachments and the extinction of all desires—even those motivated by the moral affects—and their replacement with detachment. In principle, at least, that transformation occurs in the following ways. If in the meditation experience, the meditator becomes fully aware that with respect to any of his attachments, "This is a tie, in this there is little happiness, little enjoyment, but more of pain, this [attachment] is a fish-hook" (*Khaggavi-sānasutta,* 3:27), then armed with that insight, the attachment is broken.

Again, if in the meditation experience the meditator becomes fully aware that the self is illusory—that there is no "I," "me," or "mine" to which any experience can be attached—then no desire is experienced by him as "my" desire and no gratification of any desire is experienced as "my" pleasure. Having arrived at the realization that, in effect, he can no more receive pleasure from what (out of ignorance) are called "my" desires than from what (also out of ignorance) are called "yours," all desire is extinguished.

With the attainment of wisdom, deliverance from suffering has finally been achieved—and, let it be noted, by one's own efforts. In the first place, suffering will no longer take place in this life due to the fact that all desire has been replaced with detachment; in the same way, illness, old age, and death will not cause suffering because none is now connected to anything that is experienced as "I" or "me." Second, and much more important, deliverance has been achieved from suffering in any future life because inasmuch as rebirth is caused by desire, with the extinction of desire (including the desire for rebirth), the Wheel of Rebirth has come to a halt and nirvana has finally been attained.

I have completed my summary of the Buddhist images of man, nature, and the supernatural insofar as they relate to the Buddhist message of salvation. That such an austere message should have swept up the entire Eastern world, marking Buddhism as one of the most successful missionary religions of all time, seems scarcely credible in the light of what we know about other religions. While other religions proclaim at least one creator God, Buddhism denies the existence of any. While others teach that man has at least one soul, as well as a self, Buddhism rejects these propositions. While others propose that happiness consists in the gratification of at least some desires—though they differ regarding what those desires might be— Buddhism insists that desire, any desire, can only bring suffering. While others hold up eternal life as the goal of salvation, Buddhism proclaims that salvation consists in release from any and all forms of life—in the forms, at least, that we ordinarily conceive of it. While others provide man with a supernatural savior, Buddhism teaches that in the quest for salvation man can rely on no one and on nothing but himself.

Here, then, is a salvation religion that is not just another variant of a universal culture pattern. Rather, it is one which in the configuration of its images of man, nature, and the supernatural seems to be all but unique. If, then, religious systems can be viewed, as many students of religion do indeed view them, as mirrors that reflect man's nature—if not his nature as it is, then the one he aspires to achieve in his highest moments—it must be remarked that Buddhism supports the theory of the cultural relativity of human nature in its most exaggerated form. The contrasts I have just drawn between the Buddhist images of man, nature, and the supernatural and those of other salvation religions would seem to suggest that men have no nature, they only have cultures; and the power of these is so strong that our culturally constituted beliefs become second nature.

That, at least, is what appears to be the case from those contrasting images. But appearance is not always reality, and in this case there is a double reason for making this hackneyed observation. In the first place, the Buddhism that conquered Tibet and Mongolia, Vietnam and China, Japan and Korea is to the Buddhism that I have described in this lecture what medieval Catholicism is to New England Calvinism. With its gods and saviors, priests and redeemers, magic and masses, Mahāyāna Buddhism bears little outward resemblance to the Theravāda doctrines of man, nature, and the supernatural that have been outlined in this lecture. In short Mahāyāna Buddhism, at least, is indeed merely a variant of a universal culture pattern.

Even more important for my present purpose, the Theravāda doctrines that have been outlined in this paper are the doctrines that are found in the texts of Theravāda Buddhism. However, those doctrines are very different from the beliefs that are found in the minds of Theravāda Buddhists, as recent anthropological investigations in Burma (Spiro, 1970), Sri Lanka (Gombrich, 1971), and Thailand (Tambiah, 1970) have shown. Indeed, the similarities between the beliefs of Buddhists and those held by other religionists are, if anything, much greater than their differences. That is hardly surprising. In all the great world religions there is a discrepancy between official doctrines and the beliefs of their devotees. Such a discrepancy is especially to be expected in the case of Buddhism inasmuch as it originated as a religion of, and its texts were written by, religious virtuosi whose doctrines would hardly be presumed to form the basis for the mass religion that

Buddhism soon became. Hence although many of the normative doctrines outlined in this lecture are also the beliefs of contemporary Buddhist vir- tuosi—mostly monks, and then only some of them—they are not the beliefs of ordinary Buddhists.

Ordinary Buddhists, as anthropological research has shown, view the frustration of desire, rather than desire itself, as the cause of suffering; and rather than wishing to extinguish their desires, they hope to gratify them. Moreover, instead of rejecting the notion of a self or soul, they believe in its existence, as well as in its persistence from rebirth to rebirth. Consistent with these doctrinal shifts, rather than aspiring to be liberated from the Wheel of Rebirth, ordinary Buddhists aspire to remain on the Wheel.

As for nirvana, those for whom it is a soteriological goal do not view it as extinction, either of life or of existence. They instead view it as a kind of super-heaven in which all wishes and desires are immediately and perpet- ually satisfied. And those who view it as extinction, in either meaning of "extinction," do not desire it: they either reject it out of hand as a soterio- logical goal, or they rationalize their nonnormative view by saying that they are merely postponing their wish for its attainment. As mere "worldlings," so they explain, they have not yet reached that advanced stage of the Path where one acquires the necessary attributes of character (*pāramitta*) to de- sire such a goal, but they hope to acquire such attributes in a future rebirth. In the meantime, they—like those who reject nirvana—have a different im- age of salvation, one in which they are reborn either in this world, as rich human beings—specifically, male—or in one of the material heavens, as blissful gods. Their image of salvation is almost identical with that ex- pressed by a pious Burmese Buddhist, following the performance of an act of merit, almost ten centuries ago.

> Meantime, before I reach Nirvana by virtue of this great work of merit I have done, may I prosper as a man, and be more royally happy than all other men. Or as a spirit [god], may I be full of colour, dazzling brightness and victorious beauty, more than any other spirit. More especially I would have a long life, freedom from disease, a lovely complexion, a pleasant voice, and a beautiful figure. I would be the loved and honoured darling of every man and spirit. Gold, silver, rubies, corals, pearls and other lifeless trea- sure, elephants, horses and other living treasure—may I have lots of them. By virtue of my power and glory I would be triumphant with pomp and ret- inue, with fame and splendour. Wherever I am born, may I be fulfilled with noble graces, charity, faith, piety, wisdom, etc., and not know one speck

of misery; and after I have tasted and enjoyed the happiness of spirits, when the noble law of deliverance called the fruit of Sanctity blossoms, may I at last attain the peaceful bliss of Nirvana. (Ray, 1946:165)

Finally, rather than relying on their own efforts to achieve a happier rebirth either on earth or in heaven, ordinary Buddhists rely on the redemptive powers of the Buddha. Many of them, as Gombrich has shown for Sri Lanka, not only believe the Buddha to be alive, they view him as a personal redeemer who, by forgiving their sins, can assure them of a happy rebirth. Although most Burmans do not share that view, they (like the Sinhalese) do believe that the Buddha has redemptive power. In accordance with Buddhist doctrine, they believe that a happy rebirth is best achieved by creating merit. They also believe, however, that the most effective form of merit is created by acts of giving (*dāna*)—not any kind of giving, but giving to the Buddha, the symbols of the Buddha, and the representatives of the Buddha. Concretely that means the construction and repair of pagodas (which contain the relics of the Buddha), the construction and repair of monasteries (whose resident monks are the "sons" of the Buddha), the donation of Buddha images to pagodas and monasteries, and the making of offerings to the Buddha and to Buddhist monks. In short, the Buddha, together with his symbols and representatives, comprises what Buddhists call a "field of merit," a field with vast redemptive power; indeed, it is because the above acts of giving harness that power that a happy rebirth can be achieved.

To summarize this discussion, if we look at the beliefs held by ordinary Buddhists, we find a set of images of man and the supernatural that, rather than being unique, as the images found in the doctrines of the Buddhist texts seem to be, are instead just another variant of a universal culture pattern. This suggests that human nature is not all that relative after all. Indeed, given the similarities between the Buddhist and non-Buddhist variants of that pattern, the discrepancies between the doctrines of Buddhism and the beliefs of Buddhists indicate that culture does not form a parochial human nature in its image. Instead, there is a transcultural human nature, which transforms culture to correspond to its cognitive orientations and motivational dispositions. Although anthropology has recorded numerous instances of such transformations, this one is particularly impressive because the same transformation occurred in contexts as different as China and Cambodia, Japan and Burma, Tibet and Sri Lanka.

This is not to say, I hasten to add, that the transcultural cognitive orientations and motivational dispositions of human nature are the product solely of man's common evolutionary history, though surely that is part of the story. In addition, they are probably the product of common features of human sociocultural systems. Since those systems, however, are probably the adaptive consequences of man's common evolutionary history, I shall conclude by observing that even in his religions man does not entirely transcend his hominid biological heritage.

REFERENCES

Cowell, E. B., ed.
   1957 *The Jātaka*. London: Luzac and Co.

Davids, T. W. and C. A. F. Rhys, trs.
   1917 *Dialogues of the Buddha*. London: Oxford University Press.

Fausboll, V., tr.
   1881 *Sutta-Nipāta*. Oxford: Clarendon Press.

Gombrich, R.
   1971 *Precept and Practice*. Oxford: Oxford University Press.

Ray, N.
   1946 *An Introduction to the Study of Theravāda Buddhism in Burma*. Calcutta: Calcutta University Press.

Spiro, M. E.
   1970 *Buddhism and Society*. New York: Harper and Row.

Suzuki, D. T.
   1963 *Outlines of Mahāyāna Buddhism*. New York: Schocken Books.

Tambiah, S. J.
   1970 *Buddhism and the Spirit Cults in North-East Thailand*. Cambridge: Cambridge University Press.

Welbon, G. R.
   1967 *The Buddhist Nirvana and its Western Interpreters*. Chicago: University of Chicago Press.

TOWARD A
CONTEMPORARY THEOLOGY
OF HUMAN BEING

Edward Farley

Our topic is human being. Our inquiry, then, can be called "anthropology."[1] In one sense this is a very modern concept. Human being as a theme is a mode of thought characteristic of modern times, not only in cultural anthropology and philosophy, but in theology as well.[2] When we look at the old Protestant systematic theologies of the sixteenth and seventeenth centuries, we do not find a section labeled "human being." These theologies offered a distinct treatment of human being in sections concerning Adam and Eve and the catastrophic consequences of their act; in other words, human being in original innocence and in a state of corruption. It was only later—the nineteenth century—that both philosophy and theology presented their work under the rubric of anthropology.[3] Many movements in

---

[1]The term *anthropology* apparently was born in Protestant humanism and used by O. Casmann in 1596. Its meaning at that time was broad, referring to the study of the twofold nature of the human being. See Michael Landmann, *Philosophical Anthropology* (Philadelphia: Westminster, 1974) 17-18.

[2]Michel Foucault, perhaps the most eminent and influential French philosopher of our day, has presented a book-length historical argument that human being, a concept correlated with human sciences, is a product of recent history and may be replaced as history develops other modes of thought. See *The Order of Things: an Archaeology of the Human Sciences* (New York: Random House, 1970).

[3]Thus mid-nineteenth century works in systematic theology began to collect various doctrines pertaining to human being under the general rubric of "anthropology." On the Lutheran side, Karl von Hase's study-book, *Hutterus Redivivus oder Dogmatik der evangelisch-lutherischen Kirche* (1833), offers a section on *anthropologia* that discusses "state of integrity" and the state of fallenness of human being. On the Reformed side, Charles Hodge of Princeton entitled the second book of three-volume work on dogmatics, *Anthropology*, 1871.

twentieth-century philosophy and culture have conspired to produce what is called philosophical anthropology and also theological anthropology.[4] Any full historical account of the modern thematization of human being would have to consider renaissance humanism, Descartes' "turn to the subject," the birth of the sciences of the human being in the Enlightenment, romanticism, and European philosophical movements such as phenomenology, existentialism, and hermeneutics.

In another sense human being is an ancient and modern theme of human reflection. It was the central subject matter of some ancient philosophies (Stoicism, Epicureanism) and an important element in the great movements marching under the banners of Plato and Aristotle. Furthermore, the religious movement of the ancient world gave rise to what Paul Ricoeur calls comprehensive "myths" that describe the origin, bondage, and destiny of the human being.[5] We can then speak about a vision of human being that arose in connection with the faith of Israel (the Adamic myth) and with Christianity. The characteristic Christian view of the human being—as it comes down to us from former times and in its classical form—is a mixture of doctrines produced by a literal interpretation of the Adam story with psychologies and ontologies of Hellenistic philosophy. This anthropology, which so richly weaves together symbols of innocence, the fall, and collective guilt, Hellenistic modes of thought, widespread cultural forces like patriarchalism, with a salvation-history framework is the work of the great theologians of the past: Augustine, Boethius, Aquinas.

No one will be surprised to hear that this ancient Christian theological vision of human being is now under siege. The very essence of the vision itself is not at all self-evident to the modern world. Criticisms accumulate from philosophies, sciences, and culture loyalties that address every aspect of this vision: the original innocence of human being, universal corruption, personhood, and the possibility of redemption. Are we to permit the metaphor of siege and embattlement to determine our response? If we do, we will be content to occupy the castle of the inherited Christian view of human being and prepare our defenses. This response assumes that the work of the

---

[4]For a brief account of the history and literature of philosophical anthropology, see H. O. Pappe's article, "Philosophical anthropology" in *The Encyclopedia of Philosophy*, vol. 6. The most accessible general work on philosophical anthropology to the English reader is probably Landmann, *Philosophical Anthropology*.

[5]Paul Ricoeur, *The Symbolism of Evil* (Boston: Beacon Press, 1969).

great theologians is a once-for-all accomplishment and its product lies beyond criticism as something simply to be believed. That work, like all theological work, was itself born in dialogue with critics both in and out of the church community. The Christian view of human being is not so much a piece of timeless dogma resting above history as a loosely connected collection of insights that continually calls for reformulation. These insights are capable of being criticized by and of criticizing the world in which they occur.

This dialogical relation says two things about this Christian view of human being. First, since it is not an infallible absolute but a theological work, it can and must be criticized and reformulated. Hence it can and must listen to its critics, including its contemporary ones. The contemporary critics of the Christian vision of human being, from the architects of social liberation to the new philosophical anthropologists, may have a legitimate part to play in its theological reformulation. Second, if this vision of human being is not simply an antiquarian thing but contains insights into truth and reality, it should have something to say to its critics, to the world and culture of its day. It can critically interrogate that culture and call for its critics to listen and to understand.

I shall not attempt in what follows a comprehensive account of either this total Christian vision of human being or of the assaults on it by various factions of modernity. Instead, I shall isolate three crucial areas where the Christian approach to human being and modern critics seem locked in unresolvable conflict. The three themes are human being as soul, human being as sinful, and human being as a universal condition. I want to argue that in all three areas the inherited anthropology needs criticism and reconstruction, and on the other side, that all three areas offer important correctives to the culture and time in which we are now living. I hesitate to make such a claim. For that claim can be easily associated with those who are now using litigation to press on the broader culture what they regard as Christian views. Views of the human being that lay claim to being Christian are now before the public in the debates over abortion, evolution, and prayer in public schools. At stake in some of these debates is whether our society should write into its laws the tenets of one of its religious faiths, thereby giving state sanction to that faith. I mention this only to deny that I have this sort of thing in mind when I say that a Christian view of human being has something to contribute to contemporary culture. The way I would make this case is not by citing the authorities Christians adhere to, but by setting forth a truth that has a public character, a truth about human being which, when it is uttered, elicits the response, "Yes, we human beings are like that." This assumes that a theology of human being is not utterly private, not utterly invisible, but has some public character and import and thus can be the subject of a public forum. We shall look, then, at three ways in which the Christian vision of human being is at odds with widespreading currents of modern culture. In all three of those themes the Christian vision is properly challenged and criticised and needs reconstruction, and at the same time, challenges and corrects its challenges. It is this two-way dialogue I shall examine in connection with three themes of the Christian vision of human being. The three themes are human being as soul, human being as sinful, and human being as a universal condition.

I

The Salvation of Souls
and the Liberation of Peoples

Few would question the claim that the individual person has a special place in the Christian vision of human being. Some would even say this is the revolution of thought that Hebraic religion and Christianity introduced into the ancient world. The Psalms and Wisdom literature of the Hebrews track the agonies and ecstasies of the human heart. In those pages individuals cry out in despair, joy, guilt, shame, wonder, perplexity, and peacefulness. These cries echo down the centuries in great autobiographical works (Augustine, St. Francis), in Christian mysticism, in the existential reflections of Luther, Pascal, and Kierkegaard, and in the soul-searching of European Pietism and English and American Puritanism. This individual, personal element of theological anthropology has, like everything else, been subjected to historical scrutiny.[6] I shall not attempt a historical survey of this central motif of the Christian vision of human being, but I shall describe a few ways Christendom has given it expression. For most of the twenty centuries of Christendom, human individuality was expressed in the language of *soul*. Soul, a term found in both Hebraic literature and in clas-

---

[6]An earlier work on the subject is J. V. Langmead Casserly's *The Christian in Philosophy* (London: Faber and Faber, 1949). Casserly offers a history of what he calls the "singular," his term for individual personal existence. A recent thematization, partly historical and partly conceptual, is David H. Kelsey's "Human Being," in Peter C. Hodgson and Robert H. King, *Christian Theology: An Introduction to Its Traditions and Tasks* (Philadelphia: Fortress Press, 1982). Kelsey's category is "persons."

sical Greek, was used as the unifying term for the human self or person.[7] Although soul was thought of as immortal and capable of surviving the body's corruption, the soul alone was not human being in its full reality. Hence soul and body had to be restored to each other in the resurrection.

In addition, classical Greek philosophy used soul to express what we now would call personhood. A human being with soul indicates one who perceives, senses, thinks, purposes, feels, and wills freely. Soul is used as a unifying term for these activities and dimensions of the human person in both medieval psychology and in the sophisticated Lockean psychology of Jonathan Edwards. Although this meaning of soul cannot be easily discovered in biblical literature, it need not be thought of as utterly contradicting biblical views of human being. In the hands of the classical theologians, soul served as a term to express the uniqueness, importance, and personhood of human being. Both biblical and postbiblical authors lay claim to something about the human being that is unreducible to materiality, to the human collective, to the laws that rule the domain of magic and demons, to the laws that govern nature. This something was even unreducible to God, something that he honors and does not violate.

The point so far is that the Christian vision of human being has as one of its elements the human being as person. But something else needs to be in the picture if we are to discern how modernity challenges the vision at this point. This second element is that this focus on the individual's agonies and ecstasies determined how salvation was conceived. A paradigm of salvation arose from this focus on soul and person so that salvation meant the salvation of the soul. We are all familiar with this paradigm. Since the soul was immortal, salvation meant the securing of the soul in an eschatological and beatific condition. Because that condition was the one, true destiny of the soul, human organic and historical life is the occasion for obtaining the ultimate salvation of the soul. If this is the case, the aim and purpose of

---

[7]The term as such has no single meaning. It seems to mean in Hebrew simply a living, breathing being. In folk religion of Homeric, Roman, and medieval times it refers to a naturally immortal substance that survives the body on death and retains enough individual personality to experience the afterlife. In ancient philosophy, especially its more Aristotelian line, it is the purposive (*entelechaic*) principle or aspect of the body. As such, soul is what unifies all the various powers (*dynameis*) or faculties such as perception, sensation, thought, and feeling. Classical Christian theology synthesized the folk religion and Platonic strand with Aristotle; hence soul stood for something naturally immortal and separable from the body, but having the various faculties proposed by Aristotle.

morality, discipline, and ritual is to produce just that. We have here, then, an individualism that governs the whole paradigm of salvation.

So far we have kept the modern world out of the discussion. The air we have been breathing blows out of the Middle Ages, the Reformation, the Great Awakening. When we do let the modern world get a word in at this point, we find its criticism to be devastating. Two quite different modern traditions mount an assault on this vision of the human being. The first is carried by modern philosophies, biologies, psychologies, and social sciences. It appears at first to be largely an intellectual criticism, an issue of what we do and do not *know* about human being. The assault is weakest when it is uninformed, when it identifies the Christian view with ancient folk religion and mythical views of soul and fails to discover the deeper issues posed by the older psychologies. It is strongest when it works from the foundation built up by these sciences. Indeed, this foundation is massive evidence for the degree to which human life is subject to social, economic, biological, and geographic conditions. The success of these sciences is not simply a victory of theory, but involves real gains in dealing with medical, psychological, and political problems of human life.

These sciences together add up to a new mode of understanding. They constitute a vast revolution of human thought, a virtual new hermeneutic. This hermeneutic is simply that things, including human being, are the sum total of their discernible conditions. Accordingly, we shall call this mode of understanding a hermeneutic of causality. Human being is what can be known about human being. And what can be known are the patterns, causes, regularities, and recurrences of behavior and events. For such a hermeneutic, human being as soul, as person, as inviolable self, as the seat and agent of subjectivity, is a relic of a former mythical and prescientific age. I indicated initially that this appears to be largely an intellectual issue between two very different visions of human being. The reason this is not the case is that all systems of knowledge and cognitive enterprises that get a hearing in society exist in correlation with institutions and social powers. Accordingly, the hermeneutic of causality is all-pervasive in modern bureaucracies, including those of government, health-care, the military, and even churches.

The second assault on the theological vision of human being does not appear to be primarily intellectual in character. It does not rise primarily from the question of what we do and do not know. It is addressed not to the initial premise of theological anthropology, the personhood of human being, but to the individualist paradigm of salvation. Because this paradigm thinks of salvation individualistically and eschatologically, it is prevented from thinking about it socially and historically. The individualist paradigm sets certain constraints, certain restrictions on thinking. Moreover, these constraints are reinforced by the institutions that enforce orthodoxy and pure doctrine in Christendom. These constraints prevent the church from addressing the way in which human misery is perpetrated by the social systems themselves. Political, racial, and sexual economic oppressions are factored out of the paradigm of salvation and with that the possibility of social liberation is lost. These constraints, likewise, prevent the church from addressing its own institutional complicity in these oppressions. The ecclesiastical institution's primary function is to support and advance the individual paradigm of salvation, and this means that it is supporting a mode of thought that works against the discovery of evil and oppressive social structures.

In saying this, I suggest another hermeneutic or mode of thought that is widespread in most of the nations of the world. This is the Marxist hermeneutic, which some have pointed out could be a valid mode of interpretation even if every single fact and tenet of Marx's own analysis turned out to be wrong. Anytime we acknowledge that certain events, organizations, or symbols are functioning in a social system to keep an interest group in power, we are thinking within this hermeneutic. The critique offered by this hermeneutic is not merely an intellectual one; it also has a moral dimension. Its charge is that the powerless, the poor, the disenfranchised of the society are maintained in that condition by the institutions and dominant paradigms of that society, one of which is the individualist paradigm of the salvation of souls.

Do these critiques of the personalist tradition in theological anthropology have any validity? I cautioned earlier against a defensive posture that merely absolutized the theological tradition and placed it beyond criticism. If theology simply repudiates these criticisms, it will find itself depicting human being as floating above the causalities of nature and history and callously ignoring the disenfranchised of the world in favor of those who have power and plenty. I shall not dwell on the issue posed by the hermeneutic of causality. The theological task it sets is how to understand human being both as soul, as person, and as subject to causalities. How can the human being both embody and transcend the patterns and causes of organic and historical life? The challenge here is not so much to give up the personal as to find a way of relating it to its conditions.

The second challenge may be more radical: it exposes problems not about the personal, but about the way the personal has set a paradigm for salvation. We recall at this point that a social element in salvation is not utterly foreign to the Christian vision of human being. This was, in fact, the primary paradigm in Hebrew religion. The wrath of the prophets was directed against the *institutions* of Israel and exposed their complicity in the corruption of Israel. That motif has risen from time to time in Christian history. But can contemporary Christendom be receptive to the hermeneutic of ideology? The question is rhetorical since many individual interpreters and some branches of Christendom do, in fact, make use of this hermeneutic. If Christendom simply repudiates that hermeneutic on behalf of its paradigm of individual salvation, it will surely be considered the religion of the powerful in the eyes of most of the nations of the world as well as in the eyes of disenfranchised populations in its own countries. This is, of course, the problem with which the so-called liberation theology is struggling.

If Christendom and Christian theology positively respond to this criticism and incorporate something of this hermeneutic of ideology, the individualist paradigm of the salvation of souls will be expanded to another paradigm. What would such an expansion entail? It would involve an expanded philosophical anthropology that goes beyond human being as soul to human being in the world and to human sociality. In this anthropology human well-being could not be formulated simply in individual terms, but rather also as something that has worldly and social conditions. Second, the vision of human corruption would be expanded from simply the individual's burden of hereditary or original sin to a theology of societal corruption. Only then would social oppression and the complicity of institutions in power (including the church institutions) become central to the agenda of the churches. As it now stands, most churches are not seriously bothered about the oppressive effects of sexual oppression or societal structures that leave people disenfranchised. They do become concerned about the individual glimmers of these things, the plight of the abused wife, the empty refrigerator and giftless Christmas of the poverty-stricken home. The individualist piety of the church does encourage compassion for individuals who suffer. So long as its paradigm of salvation is what it is, it remains in bad taste to dwell publicly on matters of social oppression, of racist, sexist, and economically exploitive societal structures.

Thus far we have entertained the possibility that Christendom take seriously the criticisms of its own vision of human being that come from the modern hermeneutics of causality and ideology. We must now ask whether theological anthropology has anything to say to the critics themselves both as modes of thought and as societal realities. One does not have to be part of social-science-oriented bureaucracies very long to sense that something is wrong. We have acknowledged that the data-oriented methods of these sciences and the institutions for their application are successful in monitoring the regularities of human life. If there is a connection between bottle-fed babies and I.Q. level, it will be noticed and formulated. However, the human being in these interpretive systems and their institutions is a composite of external relations. Accordingly, human mental or emotional disturbance is reducible to genetics and chemistry. Human evil is a matter of genetic inheritance from pre-human hominid ancestors. Human behavior is a matter of discerned rewards and punishments. What I question here is not the validity of the specific studies, of brain chemistry, of statistical correlations, but the paradigm that occurs when these causal relations define the human being. While the paradigm of causality is valid at its own level, it does omit the human being's experience of itself. Since experience is not quantifiable, it is excluded from the network of causality, and that means the human being in its true and distinctive sense is excluded.

A similar problem attends the hermeneutic of ideology, the Marxist type of anthropology. The genius of this hermeneutic is that it offers a way of uncovering the complicity of almost all facets of a society in maintaining structures of oppression. But the more it sticks to this kind of analysis alone, the more it implies that human being can be saved by a new social collective, by a new and pure economics and politics. A vast social machine is created that does not know what to do with the human being as creative, artistic, unique, private, unconforming. The plight of Soviet dissidents, the return of China to many of its older traditions, and the willingness of some European Marxists to engage in a Christian-Marxist dialogue all witness to the inadequacy of the hermeneutic of ideology as a total vision of human being.

Because of the impoverishment of these prevailing, modern ways of understanding human being, the anthropology of the Christian view has an important contribution to make. That vision, however antiquated, does have to do with human being itself. We can still read the narratives, the travails, the eloquences told in ancient texts and recognize ourselves and our plight.

We may have philosophical perplexities about the older ways of talking about the soul, but we recognize behind those ways some attempt to express something we immediately experience about ourselves: the irreducibility of feeling, the anxiety with regard to our temporality, the penetration of intellective insight. Such a vision of human being may need reworking, yet it attests to something true and real.

To summarize, the first task of a contemporary theology of human being is to formulate the personalism of the Christian vision in relation to the socially and causally oriented hermeneutics of modernity; and in connection with that, to reformulate the inherited individualist paradigm of salvation.

II
Human Sin and its
Modern Surrogates

The Christian vision of the human being is more than simply a philosophy of human nature, a set of affirmations about soul, will, personhood, and the like. An ancient story captures the heart of that vision, the story of Eden, which is not a description of human nature but an account of the human problem. It did not simply list the many specific perils of human life; it interpreted the one great problem that besets human being. All the great religions of the world offer some version, often in mythical form, of this one problem. Accordingly, these religions pose the central problem of human being as suffering, fate, finitude, or ignorance. When we consult the old Jewish and early Christian texts, we do not read much about fate, finitude or, for that matter, even suffering. They do speak a lot about something called sin. This theme pervades these texts from the Eden story to the Apocalypse. It occurs there not just as one of a number of human problems, but as the one, terrible way in which human being goes wrong. This reading of human being continued throughout Christian history and in some sense remains intact.

The Christian vision of human being is a vision of history gone wrong, of a pervasive distortion that touches both every human individual and every human institution. The vision comes down to us by a merger of the Eden story with early Christian theologies, especially Augustine. This inherited vision can be stated briefly. Human being arose in history in a state of innocence, living in the immediate presence of God. This innocence was soon marred by a primordial rebellious act. The result was that human being lost its innocence and was expelled from Eden and from the presence and knowledge of God, and these losses had a radical effect. Distortion affected human nature itself, so that instead of worshiping God, all human being can do is worship idols. Because human nature itself was affected, this loss and exile from Eden was passed along in the reproduction of species; all human beings are born into a world of lost innocence, with the inclination to idolatry and to evil. Because human beings are in fact responsible for their acts, this situation is one of guilt before God, of feeling that immeasurable punishment is deserved. I have summarized this vision without using the usual theological terms, but we all know what they are: image of God, temptation of our God, temptation of our first parents, the Fall, exile from Eden, original sin, depravity, condemnation, hell.

It goes without saying that this vision is not a widespread way of thinking about human problems in the contemporary world. Certain segments of the religious community still speak its language, but it does not characterize the orientation of scientific anthropology, psychiatry, local governments, social services, or education. The vision has long been under attack. The initial attack on it came with the European Enlightenment. This included a new historical consciousness that dismissed the Eden story as any literal account of human beginnings. New sciences of human origins and planetary history further discredited any pretensions of the old story to be an empirical-historical description. The initial theological response to this sort of criticism was to acknowledge the mythical or legendary nature of the story, but to retrieve the story as a kind of parable of a perennial temptation and fall all human beings experience. In other words, there was an attempt to maintain the vision itself minus its emphasis on human beginnings. In the nineteenth and twentieth centuries, though, two ways of portraying the human problem came in to challenge and displace the Christian vision, and these amounted to much deeper criticisms than those prompted by historical consciousness.

The first comes from a resurfacing of that tragic vision of human being that lies at the root of the hellenistic strand of the Western heritage.[8] According to this vision, human being is not an essentially good and innocent

---

[8]The "tragic" in the narrower sense will be identified with a certain genre of literature, the occasion of which is the tragic drama with its elements of fate (*moira*), hubris, nemesis, tragic hero, agents of vengeance, and so forth. The tragic drama manifests a tragic vision of the human situation. Thus Ricoeur can number the "tragic myth" as one of the several fundamental visions of the human problem and situation. *Symbolism of Evil*, pt. 2, ch. 2.

creature gone wrong. The distinction of good and evil is secondary to a more primordial condition of the human being in which the glory and accomplishment of human being are inseparably bound up with the shame and victimization of human being. Human being pays a price for its freedom, courage, self-transcendence, and imagination, namely its anxiety, suffering, pride, and violence. These two strands of human experience are inseparable because they are interdependent. One cannot have imagination (and, therefore, imaginatively project the future) without anxiety. One cannot be transcendently self-aware, sensitive to the self and to others, without suffering.

I said that this vision had resurfaced in modern times. Although it always had some representation in Western philosophical and religious movements, it is characteristic of twentieth-century continental philosophy and widely present in much of contemporary fiction and poetry. I am thinking of those philosophical currents we associate with Heideggerian and Sartrian philosophies of existence as well as the fictional works of Kafka, Camus, Conrad, Hemingway, Nathaniel West, and many others. These literatures represent a resurfacing of the Hellenic tragic vision because they trace the wrongness of the human being to human nature itself, and finally, to the way the totality of being is constituted. The world system is a pattern of events, relations, and relativities in such competition with each other that any sensitive, knowing, feeling being like human being not only is going to be caught up in the conflict but is going to be agonizingly aware of being so caught. In the tragic vision human being is problematic and wrong because that is the way the world is.

The Christian vision of human being is particularly vulnerable to the criticism implied by the tragic vision. This is because that vision formulates the sinful inclinations of the human being in such a way as to deny the constitutive nature of the tragic. This is not to say that the Christian community is unaware or insensitive to the sufferings and catastrophes of human life. A theology of those catastrophes is, in fact, part of the Christian vision of human being. The way it fits into that vision has to do with the relation between sin and suffering, sin and catastrophe. In the traditional, inherited version, suffering and catastrophe are simply the results of sin; the primordial fall introduced them into the world.

This means, then, that there is nothing about the world, about created being, or about finite human being, that evokes suffering or catastrophe. And if suffering and catastrophe owe their existence to the fact that the world has an *accidental* character, then the Christian vision appears to be denying the accidental character of the world. Furthermore, its explanation of suffering and catastrophe appeals to a literalization of the Eden story, an interpretation that says suffering and catastrophe were introduced into planetary history after a specific event in human history. Such a view is contradicted by such an overwhelming mass of evidence as to be simply discredited. Hence the truly profound and realistic vision of human being is the tragic vision. The Christian vision of fallen human being appears to be a relic of a discredited past.

The second comprehensive way of thinking about the human problem that contradicts the Christian vision is *therapeutic*.[9] If the resurfacing of the tragic is primarily a literary phenomenon of universities and intellectual movements, therapeutic is a widespread and popular cultural movement. According to Phillip Rieff, the coming of therapeutic as a type of culture and mode of interpretation is also the coming of a type of human being, psychological man. There are close relations between this development and what we called the hermeneutic of causality. One element in therapeutic is an understanding of human being as the result of a nexus of causes: biological, social, psychogenetic, etc. Therapeutic is distinctive in that it puts these things together in a comprehensive interpretation of the human problem. Based on that interpretation, the human problem is due to the damaging effects of either heredity or environment on the human psyche. The model at work in the background of this approach is a medical model, although some expressions of therapeutic are closer to that model than others. The human problem is a pathology, a damaging of the human being in ways analogous to injuries and diseases. This is why the answer to the human problem is therapeutic, a process (chemical, psychological, interpersonal) whose primary metaphor is that of healing.

Although therapeutic is a widespread popular movement, it does have an extensive literary expression. Some of this literature is offered by the major schools of psychotherapy that offer their analyses as total *Weltanschauungen*—comprehensive conceptual frameworks for interpreting the human being and addressing the human problem. Hence, Freudianism,

---

[9]"Therapeutic" is used here as a term for a comprehensive cultural movement, not a specific medical or interpersonal method of treatment. This is the meaning offered by Phillip Rieff's seminal study, *The Triumph of the Therapeutic: Uses of Faith after Freud* (New York: Harper and Row, 1966).

neo-Freudianism, Gestalt therapy, and reality therapy build upon a scientific, theoretical basis for a therapeutic. A less rigorous but more popular type of literature emphasizes self-development. On a different spectrum, approaches to therapeutic range from the medical model on one side (as in traditional psychiatry) to more humanistic psychologies that attempt to transcend the medical model (as in Laing or Thomas Szasz).

The challenge to theological anthropology offered by therapeutic is closely related to the criticisms of the hermeneutic of causality. It is different only in that it applies a more causal type of analysis to the human problem. In its view the human problem is largely a matter of victimization by internal and external forces beyond human control. This is why the therapeutic version of human redemption places the emphasis on processes that either change the environment from which those forces originate (such as modifying a pathological family structure) or help the human being create resources to deal with these forces. Accordingly, from the therapeutic point of view, theological anthropology is blind to the enormous power of the involuntary aspects of life and to the power of events to victimize human beings. Proponents of the therapeutic method suspect that the preoccupation with sin, idolatry, and moral guilt is a remnant from some ancient mythology of punishment now discredited by modern psychological and biological wisdom. In the therapeutic world, human actions are not morally wrong. They are risky, gross, impractical, neurotic, politically unfeasible, manipulative, insensitive, narcissistic, naive, but not wrong.

We pose the same question to these challengers of the Christian vision of the human problem that we posed to the challengers of the mythos of salvation. Does theological anthropology have anything to learn from and to contribute to these challenges? We begin with the first part of the question. Does the Christian vision of human being need to be modified by the tragic vision and by therapeutic? I would submit that it very much needs to incorporate the tragic vision. There are hints of a tragic way of looking at things even in the old texts—Ecclesiastes, for instance. But these remain only hints, with little use made of them in the history of Christendom. In point of fact, theological anthropology entertains a very serious problem once it acknowledges the Enlightenment demythologizing of the Eden story. If it gives up the claim that once upon a time there was a primeval utopia occupied by an utterly innocent and ambiguously good set of first parents, how does it account for the origin of sin and historical corruption? Does it hypothesize that all human beings are really pure and innocent, but that purity somehow transforms itself into evil? Or does it simply submit to the

Manichean view that human being is intrinsically evil, virtually capitulating to the tragic vision?

Here, theological anthropology would do well to listen to the voice of the tragic tradition. For if we acknowledge that there is in the very constitution of the world and finite human being a tragic element, then we do not have to think the impossible, namely that human being underwent transformation from some state of utter purity to a state of sin. In the tragic view, limitation and ignorance force human being to exist in the mode of anxiety and suffering. Quite simply, one cannot be a self-aware, organic being living amidst the dangers of organic life without anxiety, suffering, and fear. It is just this tragic situation that is the matrix of sin. Unable to tolerate this constitutive anxiety and fear, human being tries to secure itself in an absolute way.

As to therapeutic, surely Christendom cannot pretend that its own vision of human being is an exhaustive account of the human problem. Even as it needs to learn from the hermeneutics of causality that human beings are shaped by their social and biological environments, so it must discern how causalities and conditions create the human problem. There *is* a victimizing element in human life, and the uncovering of it and of ways of dealing with it is the contribution of authentic therapeutic. Because it does not comprehend social victimization, Christianity too quickly lends itself to an individualistic moralism that ignores the social aspects of redemption. Since it fails to grasp biological and psychological victimization, it frequently interprets such matters as homosexuality in utterly moralistic and legal terms.

I move now to the second part of the question: Does the Christian vision have any contribution to make to a culture that sees the human problem in largely therapeutic and tragic terms? Any positive answer to this question assumes that something of that vision survives criticism. If we acknowledge the force of the Enlightenment demythologizing of the inherited doctrine, then we face the task of reconstructing this vision of the human problem.[10] What survives the Enlightenment criticisms of the precritical

---

[10]Such a retrieval and reconstruction is just what is occurring in the theological anthropologies of a number of twentieth-century theologians. One of the most well known is Reinhold Niebuhr's Gifford Lectures, *The Nature and Destiny of Man* (New York: Scribner's, 1941-1943). Also significant are a number of works by Karl Rahner, which constitute a reconstruction in theological anthropology. For instance, *Hearers of the Word* (New York: Herder and Herder, 1969); *Spirit in the World* (New York: Herder and Herder, 1968); *Foundations of the Christian Faith* (New York: Seabury Press, 1978) chs. 1-3; and *Hominisation; The Evolutionary Origin of Man as a Theological Problem* (New York: Herder and Herder, 1965).

elements in the theological vision of human being is a set of rather distinctive insights into what besets human being.

Since we human beings experience ourselves in modes of limitation, suffering, and catastrophe, it is self-evident but not very profound to say that the risks and miseries of organic life are what beset us. If we entertain this self-evident theme of human suffering with the aid of the tragic tradition, we discover that life is not only risky, anxious, and painful, but that it is especially so for beings with imagination, self-transcendence, and intellect; in short, with human being as soul. As modern representatives of the tragic tradition tell us (Heidegger, Tillich), anxiety constitutes the essence of human being. The world is a scary and insecure place, and it is scarier for beings who can generalize and express that feature in symbol and language. If stopped here, this would be tragic anthropology. However, it is exactly here that the distinctiveness of the Christian vision begins.

According to the Christian vision, this perilous and insecure situation is not itself the human problem. It only evokes from human being a response to it, a way of handling it, which introduces an irreversible distortion in human being. Beset by the perils of existence, human being begins looking for that which will remove those perils. The one place there is to look is simply the surrounding world, the environment in which human being lives in the first place. Because of our imagination and self-transcendence, we human beings live in the world through language and symbols, by which we assign meaning to objects. We can and do mean things in different ways, as important or unimportant, as ugly, beautiful, trivial, useful, and so forth.

When we are drawn to things around us for the sake of finding in them some security against our misery and peril, a very distinctive use of meaning arises. The perilous nature of existence is a problem of an absolute character; insecurity besets us simply as finite beings, as creatures. To search for something to cure that, to secure us against that, is to look for something that will remove our very creatureliness and make us invulnerable. So when we assign that kind of significance to something in our environment, we are virtually saying, "If this thing can remove our creatureliness and really secure us, it itself must not be vulnerable." This very distinctive act gives the world or things in the world (events, persons, nations, causes, symbols) an absolute character. Mentioning this comes close to the heart of the theological vision of the human problem. It says that this strange act of self-securing, of absolute attachment to mundane things, has so pervaded the activities, institutions, and religions of human beings, that a vast distortion is introduced into human history. Absolutizing attachment becomes the human way of being-in-the-world.

A third step of the reconstruction shows how this absolutizing attachment is itself responsible for what we identify as human evil, for things like greed, malice, fanaticism, various violations of other persons, and so forth. Once that is done, there is a description of human wrongness that is both a bondage (because it is part of history) and a freedom (because we contribute to it out of our self-determination). What is set forth here is, I think, the vision of human being found in the Eden story, in the Old Testament prophets, in the Pauline theology. Its language is exile from the garden, sin, idolatry. As a perennial feature of human history and of individual existence, it is not reducible to the tragic structure of organic, human life. That structure is there, but as the background and presupposition of sin. It is a different kind of phenomenon from the victimizations that therapeutic worries about. This vision, therefore, charges a culture dominated by tragic and therapeutic categories with not going far enough in depicting the human problem, with a certain superficiality in discerning the distortions at work in human being-in-the-world.

III

Theological Anthropology and the Contemporary Assault on Ontology

I have reserved for last what may be the most radical challenge of all. Like the social and causal hermeneutics, the tragic tradition, and therapeutic, the movement that offers this criticism does not see Christian theology as its primary target. The movement I am referring to could be described as the most recent stage of continental phenomenology. This means both the late Heidegger along with his followers, and in France the successors of Sartre and Merleau-Ponty, namely Michel Foucault and Jacque Derrida.[11]

---

[11]Although sometimes associated with the structuralist movement, Foucault and Derrida are best thought of as the center of their own typical approach, called by some "deconstructionism" because of their method of deconstructing language. Foucault is presently a professor of the History of Systems of Thought in the College de France, Paris. Most of his major works are now translated into English. In addition to his historical "archaeologies" and "geneaologies" of medicine, insanity, prisons, and sexuality as culturally created institutions, he has written *The Order of Things: an Archaeology of the Human Sciences* (New York: Vintage Books, 1973); *The Archaeology of Knowledge* (New York: Harper and Row, 1972); and *Language, Counter-Memory and Practice* (Ithaca: Cornell University Press,

We could add to this list the Frankfurt School of critical social theory.[12] The one thing all of these figures have in common is the repudiation of what they call "ontology." There is nothing new about such a repudiation. Frequently that has taken place as a criticism of "metaphysics," by which is meant the speculative tradition in philosophy. An antimetaphysical temper characterizes positivism, logical empiricism, analytic philosophy, and pragmatism. But something is occurring in these repudiations of ontology that goes beyond the criticism of the speculative tradition. Ontology, to the degree that it can be distinguished from metaphysics, need not be a speculative enterprise. It need not entertain the question of why there is something and not nothing, questions of the nature of being, of the ultimate, most real entities, and so forth. Ontology can limit itself to the discernment of regions of manifestation, to descriptions of the persisting and intrinsic features of nature, history, art, human being. If this is the case, a repudiation of ontology goes beyond simply a criticism of speculation. It questions any cognitive enterprise that pretends to grasp intrinsic features of types of being.

Heidegger's version of the "destruction of the history of ontology" goes something like this.[13] Any attempt to discern and formulate necessary features of being, even regions of being, presupposes that being is an object, something defined against a knowing subject. It represents world or being as if it were a discrete object of a discrete science. Being, then, is objectified, studied, described much like chemical elements or the solar system. But this whole approach so distorts the matter as to lose it from the start. Being is not a persisting structure; it is a mystery, an occurrence, a "dis-

---

1977). Derrida teaches the history of philosophy at the Ecole Normale Superieure in Paris. Many of his major writings are also available in English. *Writing and Difference* (Chicago: University of Chicago Press, 1978); *Of Grammatology* (Baltimore: Johns Hopkins, 1976); *Speech and Phenomena* (Evanston: Northwestern, 1973); and *Spurs* (Chicago: University of Chicago Press, 1978).

[12]While the Frankfurt School, especially in its earlier pre-World War II period, was dominated by two major figures, Max Horkeimer and Theodor Adorno, it is known now through the works of Herbert Marcuse and Jurgen Habermas. Major works by Habermas available in English are *Knowledge and Human Interests* (Boston: Beacon Press, 1971) and *Theory and Practice* (Boston: Beacon Press, 1973). There is now a fairly large secondary literature interpreting this school and its major figures.

[13]Two small works of the later Heidegger are especially important, "The Letter on Humanism" and "On the Essence of Truth." These and other pertinent essays are available in an excellent English translation in David F. Krell, *Martin Heidegger: Basic Writings* (New York: Harper and Row, 1977).

closiveness." "Occurrence" does not mean something out there presenting itself to a sense perceiving action. That formulation returns to the objectifying posture of ontology. When disclosure takes place, we do not have a subject that first constitutes itself as subject perceiving something constituted as object. That may describe a scientific investigation, yet it does not describe the way being "happens" on the field of being, which is human *Dasein* or existence. The way to catch being, then, is not by objectifying inquiries but indirectly, in coming to consciousness about what happens in language and in thinking. The philosopher attempting this is more like a poet than a traditional ontologist, for it is the concreteness of disclosure that is at issue. Heidegger's program can be read another way, namely as itself an ontology, especially of human being.

In Foucault and Derrida we have philosophers who pick up the anti-ontology of Heidegger's late writings.[14] Foucault's anti-ontology combines a certain kind of historical thinking with the critique of ideology associated with Marxism and the Frankfurt School. As a historian of science, especially the human sciences, he sees the whole ontological enterprise as one specific, Western mode of thought that had a beginning and is already ending. In that enterprise, especially as it gave birth to modern sciences of human being, it was assumed that the world offered itself in realms of order, so that things appearing in the world could be classified on the basis of analogy. Furthermore, Foucault, like Habermas and the Frankfurt School, sees all human language pervaded by and serving prevailing institutions of power, which exercise constraints on that language. He and Derrida both are, accordingly, suspicious of any pretense on the part of human beings to describe timeless or ahistorical features of being. That sounds to them like the attempt to avoid or hurdle the determinacy, timefulness, relativity, and language of one's own time. One may in a historical way plot the relation between discourse and institutions in a given strand of time. One cannot do that as ontology.

This assault on ontology may be far more significant than is indicated by the fact that two or three contemporary philosophers are involved in it. The whole tone of contemporary European philosophy issues from this assault. If one considers that this assault combines easily with the anti-ontological tendencies of both linguistic philosophy and a technocratic culture,

---

[14]See especially Derrida's essay, "The Ends of Man," *Philosophy and Phenomenological Research* 30:1 (September, 1969).

it may be that a new consensus is in the making. But what does this have to do with theology and with the Christian vision of human being? First of all, an assault on ontology is also an assault on "fundamental ontology," an expression for a certain kind of approach to philosophical anthropology. Also, philosophical anthropology itself is repudiated as an enterprise that would discern distinctive, enduring, intrinsic features of human being. According to this movement, human being as historical eludes and transcends intrinsic features, a theme born perhaps in Sartre's argument against the concept of human nature.

This assault on ontology amounts to a criticism of theological anthropology at two levels. The first concerns theological anthropology as a distinctive theological tradition coming forth out of the patristic period through various periods of Christian theology. I pointed out earlier that this classical Christian view drew on the philosophical anthropologies of the ancient world. It appropriated the philosophical psychologies of the structure of the soul to express its own personalism. In the twentieth century theologians continue to make use of philosophy and other disciplines for the same purpose. Thus Christian theology has expressed its own humanistic element through concepts borrowed from phenomenology and existentialism. Theological anthropology is, in other words, closely bound up with the conceptual world of classical and modern ontology. The destruction of ontology seems to be also the destruction of theological anthropology.

The second level is not anthropology in the sense of the Western theological tradition but in the broader sense of the vision of human being found in the formative literature of Israel. I argued previously that there seem to be elements in the Eden story that still pertain to our human condition. This can be the case only if the elements have universal import. In other words, whatever we say about the fate of theology in its connection with Western philosophy, the vision of human being behind that has power and significance only if it is in some way universal. If that vision applied only to semitic peoples, or only to the prophetic period, it would be difficult to say how and why it has any relevance now. Because the assault on ontology is at the same time an assault on any universalizing mode of thought, it appears to be a radical repudiation of theological anthropology and the Christian vision of human being.

Does theological anthropology have anything to learn from the assault on ontology? The issue is exceedingly difficult to formulate. One reason is the ambiguity residing in the movement itself. Are we talking here about a narrow positivism unintentionally serving a society whose prevailing systems of power further their own interest by suppressing the questions of the human being and the human problem? In the case of Heidegger, we have an assault on ontology that occurs in conjunction with a startling depiction of human being and the way the world is for human being. That may not be "ontology"; but the intention of that reflection does not seem to be the elimination of human being by reducing it to a quantity or object, but the discernment of the human being/world nexus of experience. In the case of Foucault, the assault on ontology occurs in conjunction with a radical and humanistically informed critique of oppressive institutions and through sweeping depictions of historical events, epochs, and enduring institutions. The thrust of these types of anti-ontology is a caution against the assumption that the world's structures are simply written on the blank tablet of a cognizing intellect. If human being is depictable, it is not by means of explanation and classification, but by methods that retain human being's historicality. In fact, depicting that historicality is what replaces ontology in this literature.

It is just this point that must be heeded by theological anthropology. Attached as it has been to the Western philosophical tradition, the Christian vision of human being is tempted to be an additional competing ontology on the spectrum of alternatives; and yet elements of its own vision depict the historicality of human being. Hence it is understood that the human problem as sin, evil, and idolatry does not lend itself to the language of a historical essence. Christian theology has always resisted the notion that these things are essentials of human nature. At this point theological anthropology might learn from the assault on ontology better ways of expressing its own radically historical agenda.

At the same time the Christian vision of human being may be crucially important in an age dominated by an assault on ontology. If that assault means not simply a polemical attempt to depict the historicality of human being, but a suppression of the "question of human being," it cannot avoid validating powers whose interest is served by that suppression. If it means that human being can have no thematization at all and disappears as such from the language and interpretive frameworks of societies, then all ways are removed for posing questions of rights, exploitation, dehumanization, freedom, and so forth. Such a world is a world turned over to perpetrators of future nightmarish holocausts. Surely the Christian vision of human being has something to contribute to society tempted in those directions.

The reason it does is not only because of the content of its vision, the paradox of human evil and human good, but its conviction that in some sense this paradox is universal to human history. This universality may not be the universality of a timeless essence; indeed, it clearly has a historical character. That is, it describes a historical continuity that nevertheless has no single timeless and definitional status.

A brief summary of the tasks of a contemporary theology of human being is in order. Those tasks include:

1) the formulation of the personalism of the Christian vision in relation to the socially and causally oriented hermeneutics of modernity;
2) the formulation of the human problem in such a way as to incorporate but not capitulate to the tragic vision and to therapeutic;
3) the formulation of the Christian vision of human being in such a way that both the historicality of human being and the universal import of that vision are held together.

THE HUMAN BEING AS
A THEOLOGICAL ANIMAL:
A BIBLICAL ARGUMENT
AGAINST CREATIONISM

Theodore Runyon

In this lecture I will attempt first to show how human beings are inevitably theological creatures, and then to analyze how the theological impulse operative in the faith of the Hebrews, in exile in Babylon, expressed itself in the creation account we find in the first chapter of Genesis. In this account I will observe how biblical faith draws on the scientific knowledge of its time in order to express its own distinctive perspective. If this can be demonstrated, it should be applicable to the debate between creationists and evolutionists in our time.

I
The Human Being as
a Theological Animal

The interests of theologians and cultural anthropologists converge when we take as our focus the human being: that creature who has to have meaning to survive. Humans labor under the impulse to organize and order their lives, and this ordering process appears to be, if not impossible, at least much more difficult without some notion of the larger purpose, direction, and context of life. As humans we need to know how we fit into the big picture, not only to make sense out of daily life but to meet and overcome crises.

This need for meaning appears to be biologically grounded. How can such a claim be supported? The German anthropologist, Arnold Gehlen, observes that the human animal, when compared with other species, is "instinct poor," or relatively underdeveloped with regard to the multitude of instincts that guide the lives of most creatures.[1] This is not to say that we do not have instincts, or that the instincts we do have are not a powerful factor in our actions and reactions, as Nobel Prize-winner Konrad Lorenz has amply demonstrated. Nor does it deny that we learn a great deal about human behavior by examining animal behavior, as anyone who has taken a course in experimental psychology knows. Yet there is a very real difference between humans and other animals, which at first glance would seem to place humans at a distinct disadvantage. As Ernst Cassirer says, "A child has to learn many skills which the animal was born with."[2] Because of our relative lack of instincts, our lack of preprogrammed behavior patterns, we lag behind the rest of the animal world. As Cassirer observes, we fall far short of the geometric accuracy of the honey bee. In the construction of their cells, honey bees "act like a perfect geometer, achieving the highest precision and accuracy. Such activity requires a very complex system of coordination and collaboration."[3] Yet the honey bee cannot take much credit for her superior achievement; she inherited it all. It was preprogrammed in her brain, and therefore involves no special skill she has mastered. She just does what comes naturally, while you and I struggle to draw a simple circle—and never quite succeed.

If we humans are underendowed when it comes to instincts, we have been given as compensation an unusually large cranial capacity to house what has been called "that cancerous growth at the upper end of the spine," our brain. Each of us has billions of open circuits ready to receive whatever information we feed them. What this remarkable brain enables us to do, which most animals better equipped with instincts cannot do, is to extemporize; to imagine alternative possibilities; to organize the information continuously being fed to us and make sense out of it by incorporating it into the patterns already there; and to project new options on the basis of what we already know.

What does this have to do with the initial claim that human beings are theological animals? Each of us is constantly expanding the amount of information absorbed. As we are constantly bombarded with information, we are forced to make sense of it, to organize it into a whole that has coherence

---

[1]Arnold Gehlen, *Anthropologische Forschung* (Hamburg: Rowohlt, 1961) 18f.

[2]Ernst Cassirer, *An Essay on Man* (New Haven: Yale University Press, 1944) 43.

[3]Ibid., 223.

and consistency. The way we do this is by "contextualizing," by putting the new information we receive into a context with which we are basically already familiar. Yet in this process the contexts themselves constantly are being expanded and forced to take in new information that requires adjustments in perspective. Our horizons constantly are being pushed outward as we absorb more and more data; therefore, we all, consciously or unconsciously, yearn for an ultimate context within which everything has its place and everything can be understood.

Our very biological nature, which leads us to assemble ever-larger worlds of meaning, makes us seekers after the logic of God—"theologians," if you will, who must find ever more comprehensive frameworks that can do justice to our experience and knowledge. The concept of "God" is for all of us, whatever our level of sophistication, a "limit concept," that which lies at the outer boundary of our knowledge, and also beyond it, and enables our world to have coherence.[4] Put most simply, biologically we are that animal who is destined to be a theological creature, a *homo theologicus*.

Note carefully what I am claiming and, just as carefully, what I am *not* claiming. I am not yet talking about the concrete revelation of God in Jesus Christ but about the God-concept, which is as operative for Christians as for all other human beings. Therefore I am not saying that anyone with half a brain is a Christian, or that everyone believes in the Christian God, or that everyone, by virtue of being human, is a little bit saved. No, I'm simply saying that any human being "with any brains at all" must deal with the God-question. And implied in this is also the assertion that it is better to deal with the God-question consciously and openly and honestly than to be unaware that this is in fact what one is doing.

I am not saying that to believe consciously in God, or in a god, is to know everything there is to know about the ultimate context within which our lives are lived. Theologians and saints down through the ages, as well as the Bible itself, have always testified to what they call the continuing mystery of God. Because God both constitutes the outer horizon of our knowledge and at the same time lies beyond our knowledge and beckons us on into the beyond, the mystery of God continues at two levels: at the level

---

[4]Cf. Anselm's ontological argument for God as "that than which a greater cannot be conceived." *The Ontological Argument*, ed. Alvin Plantiga (Garden City NY: Doubleday Anchor Books, 1965) 3.

of what we know, and at the level of what we do not know. Speaking first from a Christian perspective about what we know, we claim that in Jesus Christ we are given a clue to the *character* of the ultimate context within which we "live, and move, and have our being." Jesus names that ultimate context "Father" and enables us to trust God as our Creator, Father and Lord, the one who reconciles us to himself through the love which the Son directs towards us. But to know this God is not to remove the mystery any more than to know another person is to remove the mystery of that person. Just the opposite is the case: the more we learn about another person, the more we discover there is to learn. And even though, through their commitment to us, we may know persons in the core of their being, in the will and integrity that is at the very center of who they are, nevertheless there is always more to learn layer after layer—for the mystery of a single human being is inexhaustible. How much more is this the case with God. The holy mystery of God grows more profound as our experience of God increases and our knowledge of God in Christ deepens.

The further out we push, the further toward the infinite we are led; the more our knowledge of the outer horizon expands, the more we become aware of the unknown that lies beyond, and the more the mystery of the beyond remains inexhaustible. To be able to name God, therefore, is not to be able to limit God. Although our knowledge grows with our constantly expanding horizon of understanding, the ultimate context is always greater. God always remains transcendent Lord. As the Psalmist cries out, "O Lord, our Lord, how excellent is thy name in all the earth" (Ps. 8).

What about the certainty that faith is supposed to bring? Does all this talk about ultimacy and mystery undermine the confidence, the certitude, the assurance that faith promises? Not at all. What remains constant in the midst of continually expanding horizons and growing understanding is the character of the *relationship* that God maintains with his creation and creatures. The Bible names the quality of that relationship "covenant." Furthermore, this reality of covenant is so central to the Bible that the Scriptures themselves are divided into the original covenant and the renewed covenant or, in the Latin, the Old Testament and the New Testament.

What is a covenant? It is a relationship of loyalty and steadfastness entered into by two parties, who vow to be solid and dependable and at the same time flexible and capable of being enriched. This is the model the Old Testament uses to characterize first the relationship between Yahweh and Israel, and then, by extension, God and all humankind. God pledged himself to Noah, to Abraham, to Moses, and elicited from his people in response a pledge of faithfulness and loyalty. According to the biblical writers, this mutual pledging is the paradigm for what human marriage ought to be.

Indeed, marriage offers perhaps the best analogy for understanding both the trustworthiness and the room for growth in covenant. In marriage two persons pledge themselves one to the other under God. Each commits self to the other in a sacred trust, and thereby they give their relationship a firmness and dependability. At the same time that bond with each other is meant to be not only ongoing but enriching. As the two persons mature in their experience and understanding, their relationship will grow and deepen as well. Assurance and security are not foreign to an expanding faith in God, but provide the psychic base, strength, and continuity that are necessary to make such growth possible. God is "the faithful God who keeps covenant" (Deut. 7:9) amidst all the changing circumstances of life.

II
How the Bible
Argues against "Creation"

Having laid the groundwork for the fundamental need of human beings to identify an all-encompassing horizon within which all the experiences of life can become meaningful, and having seen how, in the Judeo-Christian tradition, continuity is provided by the covenant relationship, we may now move to practical application and a biblical argument against creationism.

If the horizon which we confess as ultimate is not able to encompass the new information we have about reality, one of two things tends to happen: we either declare that whatever cannot fit within our present concept of God does not have to be taken seriously or does not exist; or we discover that our concept of God is not as big as our concept of reality—in effect, God suddenly seems less relevant because he no longer encompasses, transcends, and makes sense of reality as we know it. God is no longer *God*. God is no longer "that than which a greater cannot be conceived" (St. Anselm). Is there a clue within the Bible itself to an approach that can avoid these twin pitfalls and provide a more satisfactory alternative? I am convinced there is, and the remainder of the essay will spell out this third alternative.

One of the main sources for understanding the biblical view of human nature and human existence is found in the first two chapters of Genesis. Before turning to those accounts, however, it is important to remind ourselves that even though the creation stories speak of primeval history, they are not the most ancient materials in the Old Testament. The covenant traditions concerning Abraham, the fathers, and Moses are yet older. The earliest story of creation in the second chapter of Genesis is already shaped by the covenant motif: God is portrayed as entering into a covenantal relationship with Adam. What is seen here is an example of the human theological drive at work. A central hallmark of Hebrew faith, the covenant relationship with God, has been expanded outward to encompass the very creation itself, so that no part of human existence will lie outside the province of the meaning-giving covenant. In this sense Exodus really comes before Genesis, and provides the theological context within which the stories of origins and of the fathers are told, equating the God of the covenant with the ultimate source of all that is.

Turning to the creation stories themselves, Hebrew scholars have known for generations that there is not just one but two stories here, the more ancient one—the story of Adam—probably dating in its written form from the tenth century B.C., while the more recent one dates from the exile in Babylon in the sixth century B.C., and begins with the familiar words of Genesis 1:1: "In the beginning, God . . ." It is not necessary to know Hebrew in order to spot these differences. Open your King James Version and you will notice the contrasts in style between the two chapters as well as differences in the order of creation. Genesis I begins with a watery chaos; the dry land does not appear until the third day, followed by plant life, animal life, and then the creation of man and woman. In Genesis II creation begins with dry land, followed by the introduction of water, the creation of a man, plant life, animal life, and then the creation of a woman.

Scholars have also known for a long time that Genesis I bears striking resemblances to the ancient Babylonian story of creation, the *Enuma elish*, with which the Jews would have been familiar during their exile in Babylon. In the Babylonian story you will find the watery deep encountered in Genesis I, the division into the waters above and the waters below, and the same order of creation as in Genesis I. What is more interesting than these similarities, however, are the differences between the Babylonian and Hebrew accounts. And it is these differences that provide a possible clue to the reason for the writing of Genesis I.

When the Jews were carried into exile in Babylon, they brought with them a perfectly good story of creation that had probably been a part of their oral tradition since the twelfth century B.C., and written down since about 950 B.C. It begins at Genesis 2:4b with the words, "In the day that the Lord

God made the earth and the heavens . . ." That ancient story identified the primordial link between God and the first human creatures as a covenant relation. Adam was given responsibility to order the world, to "till it and keep it," to name and care for the animals, and to maintain the law of the Creator. The story said what needed to be said about covenant responsibilities, but admittedly it lacked the poetic power, the grandeur and sweep, of the Babylonian story. The Babylonians, after all, had written of the cosmic order and were the proponents of the most advanced "science" of the time,[5] and this science was what the Jewish children were learning, so to speak, in the Babylonian public schools. What should the Jews do? They could, of course set up an intellectual ghetto and try to keep their children from being contaminated by the new science. Instead they took a more courageous and biblically consistent approach. In response to this, the Hebrew priests composed a creation story that appropriated the magnificent cosmic sweep of the Babylonian story—they incorporated the science of the day— but they reinterpreted the Babylonian picture of creation in such a way as to put it within the context of the Hebrew covenant God. The facts of the new science were different, to be sure, from the traditional Hebrew story, but that evidently bothered neither the exiles nor the editors who put these two stories together in the form we have them today. It would have been simple enough to alter one story to fit the facts of the other. For them, however, it was not the facts but the relationships that mattered.

The original Babylonian story placed a decidedly different evaluation on human existence. Humans came into existence, according to the Babylonian account, because the gods became tired of taking care of the world. The lesser gods therefore invoked the high god, Marduke, to create some slaves who would assume the burdens of toil. Marduke heard their plea. He punished a lesser god, Kingu, who had been guilty of causing a revolt among the gods, by cutting his arteries and with the blood created human beings. Marduke then imposed the services of the gods upon humankind, and set the gods free to be the leisure class.[6]

This story was absolutely inconsistent with the Hebrew revelation of humankind's place within the ultimate context. The birth of Hebrew faith and of the Israelite nation occurred in the Exodus as the Hebrews were led out

---

[5]Cassirer, *Essay on Man*, 46.

[6]Norman Gottwald, *A Light to the Nations* (New York: Harper and Row, 1959) 573f.

of slavery, not into it. There was no way they could agree with a doctrine that viewed humans essentially as slaves! So while the Jewish writers accepted much of the Babylonian cosmology, they rewrote the relationships between Creator and humanity. In the Genesis I account, human beings are placed in the world not as slaves but as governors over the earth. Indeed, they are called the very "images of God," and exercise dominion and care over the earth as God does over the whole of creation. They are given responsibility for the other creatures and for the management of the fruits of the earth. Thus Genesis I defines our humanity in terms of our stewardship of the world, our show of faithfulness to the Creator for the things that have been entrusted to our care.

Now notice how the new version parallels, as far as these vital relations are concerned, the older story almost exactly. In Genesis II the man is part and parcel of the earth; he is shaped from the dust of the ground. But he receives his life through the breath of God and he is summoned to stewardship for the garden and care of the other animals. The one possible improvement Genesis I makes over Genesis II is that responsibility is given to male and female together, and not just to the man. Otherwise the relationships are basically the same in the two chapters. Although the picture of the world in Genesis I was borrowed in large part from the Babylonian cosmology, that cosmology was utilized to advance the basic Hebrew understanding of the ultimate nature of things.

Now perhaps you can begin to see my line of reasoning. If we want to take the Bible seriously, I suggest we make the Bible our model and do what the Bible does! The Bible does not dig in its heels and simply reject the new picture of the cosmos developed by the Babylonians, even though that picture differed in its presentation of the facts from the traditional Hebrew story. But it took the details of the Babylonian cosmology and put them into the ultimate context of the Hebrew covenant between God and humanity.

An objection could be raised at this point, however. One could ask, Isn't it just the other way around? Is not the covenant being set in the context of the Babylonian picture of the cosmos, and thus the Babylonians define the ultimate horizon. But such an objection both discloses our modern mindset and exposes it as inadequate. We tend to assume immensity of space and the furniture which occupies that space are more important than relationships. We automatically identify ultimacy with bigger, with a larger space. But is that not contrary to reality as we actually experience it? If you think of your own home, it is not the furniture in your house, the space, that defines you so much as the relationships, the covenants. The Jews knew this, and although for centuries they were without a space they could call their own, they still maintained their identity because that identity was given in the covenant relation. It is relations, not facts and furniture, that are truly ultimate and all-determinative.

I am suggesting that we would be wise to follow the example of the writers of Genesis I, and that is to be open to whatever modern science can tell us about the facts of the cosmos, keeping fully aware that these facts are constantly subject to revision; a description of the universe one hundred years hence will have quite another shape than the one scientific knowledge dictates at the present time. Our faith does not tie us to any one description of the world. Rather, like the Hebrews in ancient Babylon, we are free to take the descriptions most in accord with the scientific data of our time and put those descriptions into the ultimate framework of our covenant with God. To state it more simply, there is a division of labor involved. Scientific theories are attempts to discover and describe the *how* of creation, but they cannot tell us the *why* or the *what for*: that is the theological task. As T. S. Eliot's lines in "Choruses from 'The Rock' " remind us,

A thousand policemen directing the traffic
Cannot tell you why you come or where you go.[7]

The scientist's job is to sit at the intersection and count cars. There is no way the scientific approach can supply the ultimate context as long as it remains purely descriptive.

From the standpoint of the creationists, however, this is just the issue. Some evolutionists have turned evolution into a religious—albeit atheistic—dogma, into a complete world view that they promote as they teach evolutionary theory. Where this happens it can be justifiably challenged—not by attempting to discredit the science of the teacher, but by questioning the *theology*, involved in the interpretation of the ultimate context. The appropriate place for this challenge to occur is in the university, where conflicting religious philosophies are debated and examined for their cogency and ability to illumine human existence. It is unfair and inappropriate to ask teachers on the secondary-school level to enter into this debate. They are

---

[7]T. S. Eliot, *Collected Poems, 1909-1935* (New York: Harcourt Brace and Co., 1936) 191.

neither prepared nor are their pupils mature enough to understand the issues involved. Yet this debate is what creationists are, in effect, requesting. For if the Christian view of the ultimate context is presented, then in all fairness the claims of other religious groups and of atheism must be presented as well; and that is not what the creationists have in mind. Therefore, Judge William Overton was probably right when in his Arkansas decision he saw the creationist position as an attempt to use science courses in the public schools to buttress a certain Christian religious perspective.[8]

If the creationists insist on fighting the battle on the level of factual accuracy, they would put the Bible itself in an untenable position. One would then have to set Genesis I against Genesis II—was it seven days or was it one; was the order of creation dry land, water, man, plants, animals, and finally woman; or was it watery chaos, land, plants, animals, and finally man and woman together as the image of God? If priority were given to facts, the facts in these accounts conflict, and in the end would discredit the Bible. No sincere Christian wants to do this, for we desperately need the biblical understanding of the relationships between human beings, God, and the world. Indeed, the understanding of ourselves as stewards of the creation is absolutely essential if the planet is to survive. Indeed, this is one value derived from the biblical account that no scientist would wish to deny.

I will conclude with a plea to the creationists. Do not put the argument on such a level that the Bible will inevitably be questioned and even discredited by thinking young people. Take a cue from the Bible itself. Let the horizons expand to include the best information that the modern-day Babylonians can supply. Do not insist that children espouse a tenth- or a sixth-century B.C. cosmology in order to be true to their religious heritage. Whoever wishes to be loyal to God must allow God to be the ultimate context to which our minds aspire. Religion can be effective only as it is inclusive enough to integrate all of the available information without the necessity of denying or excluding any theories concerning the *how* of this universe. But this openness to scientific knowledge must be accompanied by a commitment to the rigorous intellectual task of putting the *how* within a consciously religious framework of the *why* and *what for*—as the writers of the first chapter of Genesis did—in order to enable the Scriptures once again to exercise their powerful understanding of human existence.

---

[8]*New York Times*, 6 January 1982, 1.

In conclusion, I cannot do better than to quote the French paleontologist and priest, Pierre Teilhard de Chardin, whose scientific research in the 1930s and 1940s into the facts of paleontology has been largely superseded today but whose theological insight remains as profound as ever.

Look from the [standpoint of] two thousand years of Christian experience and you will see [that] the two stars [science and religion], whose divergent attractions were disorganizing your faith, are brought into conjunction. Without mixture, without confusion, the . . . christian God will, under your gaze, invade the universe, our universe of today, the universe which so frightened you by its alarming size or its pagan beauty. . . . If you are able to focus your soul's eyes so as to perceive this magnificence, you will soon forget, I assure you, your unfounded fears in face of the mounting significance of [scientific knowledge]. Your one thought will be to exclaim "Greater still, Lord, let your universe be greater still, so that I may hold you and be held by you [in a context] made ever more intense and ever wider in its extent!"[9]

---

[9]Pierre Teilhard de Chardin, *The Divine Milieu* (London: Collins, 1964) 47.

RELIGION RETURNS
TO THE
SECULAR CITY

Harvey G. Cox

Not many years ago the world was full of dire prophesies about the future of religion. The great "sea of faith," which Matthew Arnold had once watched receding with a roar at Dover Beach, seemed to have reached such a low ebb that it would never return again. We were entering, it was said, into a post-Christian era. The influence of religious institutions and traditional forms of piety were in irreversible decline. The distinguished Italian sociologist Sabino Acquaviva wrote in his book, *The Decline of the Sacred in Industrial Society*, "From the religious point of view, humanity has entered a long night that will become darker and darker with the passing of the generations, and of which no end can yet be seen."[1]

Not everyone viewed the prospect of a religionless future with the same feelings. Preachers bewailed it, especially the erosion of spiritual influence on public morals. The latter-day children of the Enlightenment, on the other hand, greeted it as a liberation from ignorance and credulity. However they viewed it, most people accepted it as fact. Theologians began to ponder the meaning of the "death of God."

Even America, which because of the strong religious influences on its early history had stood as an exception to the global sweep of secularization, no longer appeared to be exempt. Religion was persisting here, the scholars declared, but only because it had settled for a much reduced place.

Students of religion were of the nearly unanimous opinion that whatever religion remained would have no connection with the public political realm:

---

[1]Sabino Samele Acquaviva, *The Decline of the Sacred in Industrial Society* (New York: Harper and Row, 1979) 201.

it would be restricted completely to the sphere of personal and family values. In a widely heralded article published in 1972, the American sociologist Richard Fenn said that here, as in all modern industrial societies, "a normative order based on religious beliefs and values is no longer possible." The fact that political systems in societies such as ours had achieved "considerable independence from religious control," he added, might well "reduce to near zero the level of interdependence between social factors and religious change." Consumption and political participation were what people wanted now, Fenn said, so that "cultural integration on the level of religious beliefs and values is . . . under these conditions no longer possible or even necessary for the maintenance of motivation and order."[2]

What Fenn and his colleagues were arguing was that secularization does not drive religion from modern society completely. Rather, it fosters a type of private religion that has no real function for the society as a whole. In other words, despite the upsurge of gurus and charismatic revivals, the link between religion and the public domain—politics—was gone forever.

When theologians heard these forecasts about the decline of religion, they began naturally to speculate about the theological and ethical implications. It did not seem premature or irreverent to think about how God, faith, and morality could be envisioned in a world in which at least traditional forms of religion were disappearing. The once-puzzling ideas of the German theologian Dietrich Bonhoeffer about a "world come of age" and a "non-religious interpretation of the Gospel" now appeared more plausible.[3] By the late 1970s and early 1980s, however, the ebb tide appeared to be turning. Religion seemed to be staging a comeback.

One particularly powerful symbol of the sea change occurred on 26 January 1979. On that day a green-and-white Alitalia DC-10 landed in Mexico City and the newly elected Pope John Paul II climbed down the stair and knelt to kiss the runway. I was teaching in Mexico City at the time, and I watched the pontiff's arrival on a tiny color TV screen with some friends in the San Angel section of the city. None of them found it all that significant. But I saw something click into place, the kind of sharp image that suddenly appears when a kaleidoscope is turned one more notch. Why I thought I dis-

---

[2]Richard K. Fenn, "A New Sociology of Religion," *Journal for the Scientific Study of Religion* 2:1 (March 1972): 17.

[3]See Dietrich Bonhoeffer, *Letters and Papers from Prison*, rev. ed. (New York: Macmillan, 1967).

cerned an epiphany when my companions saw only a middle-aged prelate kissing some asphalt will take a little explaining.

Mexico City—at least legally and constitutionally—is one of the most secular cities in the world. It is the capital of Mexico, and since the constitution of 1861 Mexico has been an officially secular state. Its laws controlling religion are severe. Parochial schools are technically illegal. It is against the law to wear a Roman collar or any other clerical costume on the streets. All religious properties, including church buildings, are the legal property of the state. Holding religious ceremonies—including masses—in public is prohibited. Diego Rivera's vivid murals, depicting bloated priests and armored conquistadores maiming Indians and plundering their gold, embellish the walls of official government buildings. On the surface Mexico City is the embodiment of a sprawling secular megalopolis, one of the largest in the world.

But underneath it all does Mexico City, like New York or maybe even Moscow or Peking, conceal some deeply buried religious quality, barely covered by its veneer of official secularity? Does some subcutaneous spirituality still animate not only its people but millions of others all over the modern world despite the enormous impact made by public education, scientific technology, urbanization and other allegedly secularizing forces? Furthermore, is there something in the air that has brought this dormant piety to the surface? Has the sleeping giant of traditional religion awakened? For me, the coming of Pope John Paul II, the head of the oldest and largest Christian Church in the world, to what may be the world's largest "secular city" posed all these questions in a single flash.

In their own way, Mexican politicians were impressed by the pope's arrival too. Whatever its religious significance, for them the papal journey was also a *political* event. It made them jittery. Admittedly, there seemed to be some reason for the apprehensiveness. Just a few weeks earlier another religious leader, the Ayatollah Khomeini, had returned to an allegedly secular country and displaced the whole government. No one thought John Paul II had that in mind, but officials knew that the Catholic bishops in Brazil had become the main opposition to the military regime there. They were aware that nuns and priests were cooperating with insurgent movements in Central America, just across the border. The new Bishop of Rome was an unknown quantity. The night before the Pope's arrival a queasy minor official told me he had dreamed that the Pope stood up in his open limousine, pointed to the president's palace and said, "Seize it!," and the crowds had drawn machetes and obeyed.

The Pope, of course, gave no such command. But from any politician's perspective, his visit was an enviable success. Millions of people lined the Avenida de la Reforma—named, ironically, for the secular Reform of 1861, which had resulted in the expropriation of the church's property—to cheer and wave. With blithe disregard for the anticlerical laws, John Paul II appeared everywhere in resplendent white papal garb, and celebrated mass in public. Watching the huge crowds, members of the ruling party could not help reflect on the efforts needed to cajole even small and unenthusiastic groups into attending their appearances. As the departing Pope's plane circled the city on its way back to Rome and thousands of Mexicans flashed "adiós" with tiny hand mirrors (the idea of an enterprising local glassware dealer), one could almost hear the collective sigh of relief that went up from the Palacio Nacional.

The surprising weight attached by the local politicians to the visit of a priest from Cracow who commands no divisions highlighted another issue. Not only are we witnessing a resurgence of traditional religion in the world, this resurgence has an undeniable—if still indeterminate—*political* significance.

The ambiguous character of this political dimension in religion's revival was underlined for me by two visits I made in the summer of 1982. While making a return trip to Mexico in July I stopped in Lynchburg, Virginia, to acquaint myself with the work of the Rev. Mr. Jerry Falwell, minister of the Thomas Road Baptist Church there and founder and president of Moral Majority, Inc. During my brief stay I attended the Bible Study Hour and the regular Sunday morning service at Thomas Road Baptist Church. I visited Liberty Baptist College and Seminary, also founded and headed by Mr. Falwell. I inspected the imposing headquarters of the "Old Time Gospel Hour," Mr. Falwell's widely viewed national network TV program. I talked at some length to the staff members of Moral Majority, Inc., about their efforts to enlist hundreds of thousands of Americans into bringing a conservative influence to bear on public policy in America. Mr. Falwell himself served as my affable host for a luncheon at the local Hilton Hotel restaurant. I left Lynchburg with the impression that I had met a man who personifies the most conservative side of the return of religion—both religiously and politically—one was likely to find anywhere in the world today.

A few weeks after my visit to Lynchburg I attended Sunday mass at the venerable old cathedral in the city of Cuernavaca, Mexico. The Bishop of Cuernavaca, then in his final weeks of service before his retirement, was Don Sergio Méndez Arceo, one of the most prominent voices of the "Catholic left" in Latin America. The guest preacher for the day was Father Ernesto Cardenal, the controversial priest, poet, and symbol of Christian participation in revolution. A few months later Pope John Paul II, during a visit to Nicaragua, would publicly scold Cardenal for remaining at his post as his country's Minister of Cultural Affairs. Standing next to the high altar that day in August, however, Cardenal did not appear to be a man who would be much affected by scolding. He spoke with great feeling about how Christians were becoming active in the struggle for justice all over the continent, especially in El Salvador and Guatemala. Within the span of a couple of weeks I had touched down on the two most antipodal outposts of Christianity to be found today; Jerry Falwell and Ernesto Cardenal represent the polar antitheses of the Christian world.

Falwell and Cardenal are not merely mirror images of each other. They are enormously different men temperamentally, and they occupy different places on the two wings of the religious movements they represent. Still, there are some intriguing similarities. Both underwent life-changing religious conversions as young men. Both moved from a deep suspicion of the world of politics toward finding themselves immersed in it. Both are charismatic figures whose persuasiveness springs more from personal conviction than from polished eloquence. Both take positions that sometimes embarrass their more cautious colleagues. In short, Falwell and Cardenal embody both the return of religion and its powerful but contradictory political significance as well as anyone could. Taken together, the question they pose is this: What is the meaning of the present dramatic reappearance of religion as a potent political force all over the world just when the experts had thought it was all over?

Subsequent events in the world have made this question increasingly more pressing. Shortly after the pope's visit to Mexico a band of Shiite Muslims seized the American Embassy in Teheran and held a number of its staff as hostages. Back home the average American was not only angry but confused. Having heard for years that our nation's enemies were godless atheists, they found it hard to understand bearded mullahs who called the United States "satan" and were depicted on the news as religious fanatics. Then, in December 1980, four American Roman Catholic women missionaries were shot to death in El Salvador—not, it appeared, either by godless communists or by fanatic Muslims but by soldiers carrying rifles supplied to them through the ruling junta by the United States government. Religion and politics were not only being mixed, but in highly unfamiliar ways.

Every week new evidence suggested something was astir. The Roman Catholic bishops of Canada issued a sharp criticism of their government's economic policies, claiming discrimination against the poor. The Sunday *New York Times Magazine* carried a cover article about the Protestant and Catholic churches of South Korea and their strong public opposition to the regime there.[4] The Catholic Bishop of Manila called on the businessmen of his nation to join him in opposing the Marcos government. Even in communist countries religion appeared to be assuming a more prominent public role. In Poland, members of the Solidarity trade-union movement, which was repressed by a martial law decree in December 1981, sang hymns at their rallies and carried pictures of the Blessed Virgin on marches. The leaders, including Lech Walesa, appeared to be motivated by Roman Catholic values. Visitors to the U.S.S.R. reported a growing interest in traditional Russian Orthodoxy among young people and intellectuals. Meanwhile, in February 1982 nearly four thousand youthful East Germans gathered in a Protestant church in Dresden to listen to talks by two Lutheran pastors in support of European nuclear disarmament. They met under a banner stretched across the baroque organ pipes that bore the motto "Frieden schaffen ohne Waffen" ("Build Peace without Weapons"), a phrase that directly contradicts the official East German government's position expressed by the slogan "Peace must be armed."[5]

In Western Europe also, once thought of as the epicenter of secularism, churches appeared in the public realm. A popular movement against nuclear weapons suddenly came into world visibility in 1981, and the churches—of Holland and West Germany especially—were at its core. Laurens J. Hogebrink, a Protestant pastor, often spoke for the Dutch Interchurch Peace

---

[4]Henry Scott Stokes, "Korea's Church Militant," *New York Times Magazine* (28 November 1982): 67.

[5]For descriptions of the role of the Church in Poland and in East Germany, see Syzmon Chodak, "People and the Church Versus the State: The Case of the Roman Catholic Church in Poland," in *Occasional Papers on Religion in Eastern Europe* 2:7 (November 1982): 26; James Will, "Reflections on the Role of the Catholic Church in Mediating the Present Crisis in Poland," ibid., 2.6 (September 1982): 20; Mary Lukens, "The Churches in the German Democratic Republic: Notes of an Interested Observer," ibid., 2:1.

Council. The British campaign for nuclear disarmament was led by a Roman Catholic priest, Monsignor Bruce Kent. Even in Sicily Protestants and Catholics were working together to oppose the stationing of nuclear missiles in the small city of Comiso.

In the United States the new vitality of religion in the public sphere assumed a more ambiguous form. Falwell had organized Moral Majority, Inc., in 1979, and in the fall of 1980 he and other TV evangelists—strongly hinting that they had helped elect Ronald Reagan as president—began to push vigorously for government action on restoring prayer to the schools, banning pornography, outlawing abortion, and controlling what they considered to be immoral themes in the mass media. By the fall of 1982, however, none of these goals had been attained, and nearly all candidates running on these issues lost their electoral contests. The question of how much influence political fundamentalism would have on American society remained unanswered.

Church members also began to notice a renewed series of attacks on the National Council of Churches and the World Council of Churches. They were often orchestrated by a politically conservative group called the Institute for Religion and Democracy, and their polemics focused on certain activities of these ecumenical bodies that their critics asserted did not reflect the ideas of the average person-in-the-pew.[6] But there no longer seemed to be a one-to-one correlation between conservative theology and conservative politics. In 1978 an organization appeared called "Evangelicals for Social Action," which presented itself as offering "education, support, and analysis toward biblical social change." Its statement of purpose declares:

> We are unique in that our agenda for social change is not derived from liberal or conservative social agendas, but from the scriptures.[7]

Today ESA describes itself as adhering to a "pro-life" stance on "such issues as peace and nuclear disarmament; the rights of the unborn; wealth and poverty; the sacredness of the family; the elimination of racial and sex dis-

---

[6]See *Christianity and Democracy*, issued by the Institute on Religion and Democracy, Washington DC. For a critical discussion of this group, see the 21 March 1983 *Christianity and Crisis* 43:4, articles by Leon Howell, Wayne Cowan, and the editors. See also Cynthia Brown, "The Right's Religious Red Alert," *The Nation* (12 March 1983): 301.

[7]Evangelicals for Social Action" (pamphlet), 25 Commerce Street, SW, Washington DC 20005.

crimination; human rights at home and abroad; and the protection of the environment." The influential Sojourners fellowship in Washington, D.C. took a similar political position, with somewhat more emphasis on direct action, pacifism, and the development of new forms of spiritual community.[8]

Evangelicals, in fact, were emerging as a "third force" between the vociferous fundamentalist and the establishment liberal wings of American Protestantism. As they did, they were leaving behind the posture that at least since the 1930s has made theological and political conservatism synonymous. Dr. Billy Graham, once viewed by most Americans as a streamlined version of sawdust-trail revivalism and a stalwart defender of conservative causes, had assumed a new role in his mature years. He was becoming a kind of church statesman, mediating between the various theological currents, and a vigorous critic of nuclear armament. Against the advice of the U. S. State Department, he made a highly publicized visit to Moscow in June 1982, both to preach and to attend a peace conference. He had become "ecumenical," with only the far fundamentalist right and the ultraliberal left continuing to regard him with suspicion.[9]

In 1982 the role of the American Roman Catholic bishops in the formation of public policy also took a dramatic turn. By issuing a pastoral letter on war and peace that was highly critical of American nuclear weapons policy, the bishops served notice that Catholics were not just interested in abortion or in the institutional problems of parochial schools. Monsignor Vincent A. Yzermans, who once served as information director for the U. S. Catholic hierarchy, wrote in November 1981:

> Something is stirring in the Roman Catholic Church in the United States that portends an explosion between church and state that will make the abortion issue, the school-aid controversy and the tax-exempt status of churches look like a child's sparkler on the Fourth of July. Stated simply, the church in the United States is becoming a "peace" church. . . . This revolution is being waged painfully in the hearts and minds of Catholic thinkers and leaders. . . . The American bishops are shouldering their re-

---

[8]*Sojourners,* 1309 L Street, SW, Washington DC 20005.

[9]The principal voice of the most representative evangelical body is *Christianity Today.*

sponsibility of leading this revolution, at times to the chagrin and vocal opposition of their flocks.[10]

Monsignor Yzermans emphasizes the Catholic bishops' collective support for nuclear disarmament. Some individual bishops have gone further. Archbishop Raymond Hunthausen of Seattle announced that he would withhold the portion of his income tax going for military purposes, and Bishop Leroy Matthiesen of Amarillo, Texas, has asked Catholics who work in any phase of nuclear weapons development to consider seeking employment elsewhere. In addition, the bishops have sharply criticized the U. S. policy of supplying arms to repressive Central American regimes. Although the "explosion" Yzermans predicts has not occurred, both the Vice-President and the Secretary of State have publicly questioned the bishops' policies.

By the early 1980s it had begun to look as though a revival of religion, one with important implications for political life, was underway everywhere. The old secular city just wasn't what it used to be. The evidence pointed to a resurrection of religion, and of traditional and theologically orthodox religion at that, worldwide. It appeared to be a revival, furthermore, which was not restricting itself to the sanctuary but was reaching into the barricades and the corridors of power. But there are still gnawing questions. Was it simply that the dirge was played prematurely? Was the death of God, or at least of religion, simply taking longer than expected? Are we witnessing a genuine revival of traditional religion, or is the new religious wave a creature of the mass media, or the fevered bloom on the cheek of a dying consumptive? Or is it no more than a cynical misuse of religion for extraneous purposes? If there is a genuine spiritual upsurge, why has it assumed such a political stance, and why are the political postures so disparate—revolutionary in Latin America, democratic in Poland, mixed in the United States?

In 1965, much under the influence of Bonhoeffer's theology and greatly concerned about what the expected decline of traditional religion might do to the relevance of Christianity, I wrote a book called *The Secular City*.[11]

---

[10]Vincent Yzermans, "The Catholic Revolution," *Christianity and Crisis*, 42:3 (1 March 1982): 39. For an interesting attempt to reclaim traditionally conservative symbols for a more progressive political purpose, see Joe Holland, *Flag, Faith and Family: Rooting the American Left in Everyday Symbols* (Washington: Center for Concern, c. 1979).

[11]Harvey Cox, *The Secular City—Urbanization and Secularization in Theological Perspective* (New York: Macmillan, 1965).

In it I drew upon the anticultic preaching of the Hebrew prophets and Jesus' opposition to the priestly establishment of his own day to argue that religion is not always and everywhere a good thing; secularization might not be the unmitigated scourge it was often seen to be. I suggested that instead of bemoaning the waning of ecclesial power or the disappearance of the sacral, Christians should concentrate instead on the positive role they could play in the modern world. I still believe in that thesis. The only trouble was that even as I was writing that book, the very "modern" world it sought to confront had already begun to slip into the past; a new age had begun to appear. Some called it the "postindustrial" or "postbourgeois" world, but the term most often used was "postmodern." No one was quite sure what "postmodern" really meant. But it seemed clear that whatever else it meant, the postmodern age was *not* one in which religion was going to disappear.

The current reappearance of religion does not, however, make the message of *The Secular City* obsolete. It remains true that biblical faith is often critical of human religiousness. The prophets inveigh against solemn assemblies. The religious powers of Jesus' day saw him as a dangerous threat. If secularization is not always uniformly bad, religion is not always uniformly good. If the challenge modern theology took on was to define and defend the faith in an era of religious decline, the task of a postmodern theology is to interpret the Christian message at a time when the rebirth of religion, rather than its disappearance, poses the most serious question.

What should theology say to the unexpected return of religion as a potent social force? In responding to this question, I accept the fact that theology is an "old-fashioned discipline," that it deals not just with what is, but with what ought to be. Clearly, theologians possess no monopoly on the study of religion. Historians, sociologists, psychologists, and psychiatrists roam freely through its sacred precincts as well. Still, there is a difference. When anthropologists and sociologists move as they often do from description to prescription, then we must ask: What normative vision of religion and what plumb line of its proper relation to the secular world inform their prescription? Where do they get their oughts and shoulds? As soon as they begin to answer such questions, we will have left social science and have crossed over into theology.

Theology is unapologetically *pre*scriptive. It does not claim to be value-free or neutral. Theologians draw upon the beliefs of a particular tradition to suggest a course of action, an appropriate response, a way of life commensurate with what the faith teaches. But if "modern" theology must now be superceded by a postmodern successor, where will the resources for such a theology come from? It is my thesis that these resources will come not from the center, but from the bottom and from the edge. They will come from those sectors of the modern social edifice that for various reasons— usually to do with class or color or gender—have been consigned to its lower stories and excluded from the chance to formulate its religious vision. They will come from those parts of the world geopoliticians classify as the "periphery," regions that have also been largely excluded from participation in the centers of modern theological discourse that are located in the Western political and cultural milieu.

Before the bottom and the edge can be heard from, the present weakened "center" will have to be dismantled. Not destroyed, for parts of it, such as its awareness of historical modes of thinking, will be essential to theology's next phase. Not only did Pope John Paul's arrival symbolize the return of religion with its mixed political consequences to the secular city, it also brought together the two main agents of modern theology's end: the traditional and the radical. If the new theology will come from the edge and the bottom, I believe traditional religion, in some still unforeseen combination with radical Christianity, will provide its content. In the Pope's arrival all the elements were signaled—the bottom and edge, tradition and radicality. Here the most archaic and the most avant-garde wings of Christianity appeared for a moment at least to squeeze out the middle completely. Here Poland was meeting Latin America, and Rome was kissing the Third World.

The Polish Pope is an exemplary conservative religious leader. His opposition to birth control and his insistence on clerical celibacy and an exclusively male priesthood make this painfully clear to American and European liberal Catholics. He is also a traditionalist who has made highly publicized pilgrimages to the Black Madonna of Czestochowa in Poland, Fatima in Portugal, and the basilica of Our Lady of Guadalupe in Mexico. He is a staunchly *Roman* Catholic who will not permit his interest in Christian unity to erode what he believes are the unshakable pillars of the True Faith. But in climbing out of his jet onto Latin American soil, John Paul II—the custodian of traditional religion—arrived in the habitat of Christianity's most revolutionary wing. He was stepping onto the continent where young Catholics sing a song called "The Cross of Light," honoring the memory of the Colombian guerrilla-priest, Camilo Torres; where others light candles before photos of the martyred Salvadorean archbishop, Oscar

Romero; where a Brazilian bishop, Paulo Everisto Ahrns, opened the churches of his diocese in São Paulo to illegally striking workers barred by the military government from meeting; where the highly controversial "basic Christian communities," lay-led grassroots congregations involved in Bible study and political action, are blossoming by the thousands, and the much-disputed "theology of liberation" originated.

The Pope's visit to Mexico brought the differences between traditional and radical Christianity into sharp profile. But it also revealed some elements of convergence between the two, not the least of which is their common aversion to "modern theology," the attempt to adapt Christianity to the modern world. The Pope's social pronouncements do not please conservative American advocates of supply-side and laissez-faire economics. For their part, the revolutionary Christians of Latin America are quite traditional in some ways. They puzzle moral majoritarians who prefer to believe that all revolutionaries are devoted to the destruction of monogamy and the abolition of religion. An acquaintance of mine, a priest who identifies himself with the Catholic left in Brazil, once told me that the problem with North American theologians is that they will "never understand that we Latin Americans *like* tradition and ritual and hierarchy." Liberation theologians are cautious about the use of historical critical approaches to the Bible. As for public morals, when Ernesto Cardenal became Minister of Cultural Affairs in Nicaragua after the victory of the Sandinist revolution, he immediately banned the importation of pornographic films. The meeting of the two wings of antimodernist Christianity involves consensus as well as collision.

These, then, are the two columns now engaged in ambushing the remnants of secular society and modern theology. But both wings are themselves improbable conglomerates. The conservative battalion, symbolized by the pope, encompasses both arcadian poets who loathe television and Protestant preachers who own whole networks. It includes fashionable "neo-conservatives," many of them Jewish, who write for *Commentary* magazine and whose grandmothers would light an extra sabbath candle if they knew their progeny were keeping company with Texas revivalists and Polish prelates. Still, their shock could not exceed that of the Reverend Falwell's shirt-sleeved fundamentalist predecessors upon finding a photo of a Romish Pope in a spring 1982 issue of *Moral Majority Report*. Whatever happened to "Rum, Romanism and Rebellion"?

Politics always make strange bedfellows, especially when mixed with religion. If the conservative wing of the uprising against modern theology is a potpourri, so too is the radical party. It brings together not only Latin American Catholics but an increasing number of Asian and African Christians; a growing group of feminist religious thinkers; Black American theologians; a scattering of white American inner-city Catholics and Appalachian Protestants, and—more recently—voices from the Asian-American and Mexican-American subcultures. Like the pope's division, this list includes people who until recently might have crossed the street to avoid meeting each other.

At first, the convergence of the traditionalists and radicals seems odd. The conservatives dismiss the radicals, and see their liberation theology either as a collapsing of the faith into political ideology or as just the latest sellout to modernity. The Latin Americans and their allies in the radical camp lump the sophisticated conservatives along with the fundamentalists as variations of the same religiously tinctured bourgeois ideology. But when it comes to evaluating modern theology, the two warring schools agree; they both find it a failure. Can a postmodern theology arise out of such a cacophony?

I think it will, but one should not try to answer this question at the theological level alone. Theologies, unlike philosophical schools or scientific paradigms, do not make much headway in the world unless they are borne along by vigorous religious movements. They need a social base. The emergence of a postmodern theology from the bottom and the edges of the modern world will happen only as religious movements incorporating powerful critiques of modern theology and the religious sensibility based on it come increasingly into prominence. Consequently, it is important to understand these current "religious" attacks on modern society and its theology. Only then can we adequately evaluate recent attempts to replace modern theology with something different.

Among these antimodernist religious movements, two merit special attention. The first is the dramatic reappearance of *political fundamentalism* and its recent marriage to the *electronic media* in the United States and, more recently, in other countries as well. The second is the equally dramatic appearance of the *Christian base-community* movement and of *liberation theology*, which has occurred in many places, but chiefly in Latin America.

Both movements are growing rapidly. Both are profoundly antagonistic to modern theology, especially in what they call its "liberal" or "progres-

sive" forms, though in quite different ways. Both are shattering the institutional forms of religious life that came to birth during and after the
Reformation. Both are uniting people who once fought each other and di-
viding people who once felt united. Both are creating new forms of religious association that are rendering denominations, the most characteristic
social expression of modern Christianity, obsolete. Both emphasize the Bible and claim to be recalling people to the Original Message, away from the
errors and idols of modernity. Both emphasize increased participation of
Christians in political life. Both rely on leaders whose authority has more
to do with personal charisma than with academic degrees or ecclesiastical
ordinations.

Yet despite these similarities, the differences between the burgeoning
mass-media religion of the U.S.A. and the fast-growing base-community
liberation Christianity in other parts of the world could not be greater. The
two open a schism in the church that runs far deeper than the occasional
bickering that still divides Catholics from Protestants. Mass-media fundamentalism, though it varies in tone and tenor, presents a theology that celebrates patriotism, individual success, and a political spectrum ranging
from moderately conservative to the far, far right. The base communities,
on the other hand, though they also vary immensely from place to place,
exemplify a theology that affirms social justice, the rights of the poor, a
communal understanding of salvation, and a politics that stretches from
moderately reformist to revolutionary. Still, both movements are strongly
antimodernist; to understand them is to understand why "modern religion"
and its theological rationale seem fated for dissolution.

As I have studied mass-media fundamentalism and community-based
liberation theology, asking about their influence on a postmodern theology,
it has become increasingly clear that the two are not symmetrical. Fundamentalism, at least in its early days, was putting many of the right questions
to modern theology. Conversely, the current return of fundamentalism, this
time via television and computer mailings, will probably contribute a good
deal to the failure of modern theology; but it remains too provincial, too
uncritical, too unaware of its own history. I do not believe it has much to
offer to a postmodern theology. Liberation theology, on the other hand, will
probably not play as large a role in the dissolution of modern theology (in
part because it occupies a social terrain where modern religion never gained

a secure foothold in the first place.) Nevertheless, I believe it will supply some of the main ingredients of a postmodern theology, one that combines radical and traditional, premodern and modern elements.*

---

*This material is adapted from the author's new book, *Religion in the Secular City. Toward a Postmodern Theology.* (New York: Simon & Schuster, 1984).

COMMUNITY, NATURE, AND MEANING:
THE ANTHROPOLOGICAL VISION
OF THE GOOD LIFE

James L. Peacock

A Russian factory worker was in the habit of pushing a wheelbarrow through the gate each day at quitting time. Each day the guards would inspect the wheelbarrow to see if he was stealing something. Each day they found nothing, so they let him pass. After many months, however, they discovered that the worker was stealing wheelbarrows. This story illustrates the fallacy of looking for the contents, not the container—the part, not the whole.

Probably the most salient characteristic of anthropology is holism. Anthropology strives to see history as a whole, to examine contemporary humanity as a whole, and to see life itself as a whole, in biological, cultural, and other aspects. Anthropology fails, of course, to achieve this ideal, but holism is a guiding objective; it is part of the anthropological perspective.

I will sketch this holistic anthropological perspective, especially in relation to religion. This view I shall contrast to, first, a theory, and second, a case. The theory is one that lies behind the case. It is the philosophy of individualism. The case concerns Americans, perhaps especially North Carolinians of certain cultural backgrounds, but the argument concerns America generally. This analysis addresses the question, What is the actual and what might be an ideal, relation of life to religion? What might anthropology contribute to answering this question?

We move, then, from the philosophy of individualism to the anthropological perspective of holism, then consider us, the case, and conclude with the inevitable question: wither? What vision of the good, the proper life might anthropology propose?

I
Individualism

The philosophy of individualism is familiar to us. I shall exemplify it by summarizing perhaps its greatest spokesman, the philosopher Thomas Hobbes. Hobbes's great work, *Leviathan*, though published in the seventeenth century, remains a dominant influence on our thought.[1]

In *Leviathan* Hobbes starts with the senses. How does the individual know? He senses. He sees, hears, touches, smells, thus bringing internal stimuli to bear on his external processes. For Hobbes, the senses are the bedrock of knowledge.

Here is good old Anglo-American empiricism, carried down through the ages in slogans like "seeing is believing." Even in kindergarten, children show and tell. Note the sequence: first *show*, then *tell*. Isn't that the natural way to do it? It's the empiricist way, but in some kindergartens I visited in Asia, the children don't show at all; they just tell. With us, empiricism is taught early, and why not? Isn't relying on the senses just "common sense"? What are those Buddhists talking about when they call the sensed world *maya*, "illusion"?

Back to Hobbes. Starting with the senses, he then considers the thoughts we construct from them. From the senses, we construct memories, dreams, fantasies. But these are inferior "fancies." What is memory? "Decayed sense," says Hobbes.

Hobbes also notes a way of knowing independent of the senses. This is reason. Reason is illustrated in geometry. From knowing two sides of a triangle, one can calculate the third side without seeing it. Hobbes defines reasoning mathematically. Reasoning, he says, is reckoning. You add up evidence and draw a conclusion just like a bookkeeper adding a column of figures and reaching a total.

Sensing and reasoning, then, are the basic ways to know, and it is the individual who performs both these operations. Hence the individual is the elementary unit, the atom, the building block, of society. This is the epistemological assumption of individualism.

Individuals also have a third aspect: passions. They sense and reason, but they also will and want. They want status, each other's property, and the like. This is, in Hobbes's view, human nature, the character of man in

---

[1]Thomas Hobbes, *Leviathan* (Baltimore: Penguin, 1968). Originally published in 1651.

his natural state. Unfortunately, there is only a limited amount of property and power to be had. Wanting it causes competition, conflict, even war. Man left in his natural state degenerates into a war of "everyman against everyman." (This view of human nature, incidentally, is nicely expressed in recent British literature, which still reflects the Hobbesian philosophy. Look what happens to the boys left on a tropical island in the *Lord of the Flies* by William Golding. Look at the Orcs in Tolkien's *Lord of the Rings*. And, of course, this view of human nature lies behind the so-called "law and order" advocates.) Hobbes warned that if men are left in their natural state, they will be at each other's throats, and life will be, in his famous phrase, "nasty, brutish, and short."

Human beings must therefore counter their nasty natures by introducing artificial controls. Hence they make contracts, agreements ultimately buttressed by force. Finally, they make the ultimate contract: they trade their freedom for order, which is necessary for survival. They accept the rule of someone else in order to protect themselves against others. By this a commonwealth is created, the *Leviathan*.

This leviathan is a monster, though, an artificial creation. In a picture appearing in the original edition of Hobbes's work, Leviathan is a huge man, composed of many small men, and bearing the face of none other than the sardonic philosopher Hobbes himself.

What part does religion play in this commonwealth? Religion is legitimate only so far as it reinforces the commonwealth; God must support Caesar. The final section of Hobbes's work is an unrelenting attack on a religious institution that tries to stand above the commonwealth, the Holy Roman Church. The papacy is the kingdom of darkness and the pope the prince of darkness. Why? Because the pope divides loyalty between the spiritual kingdom (what Hobbes delights in terming a "ghostly" kingdom, which he parallels to the dark realms of fairies and demons) and the secular kingdom. Divided loyalty weakens government and threatens a return to anarchy—or life that is nasty, brutish, and short.

A powerful and compelling vision! Even more powerful and compelling to read than to hear summarized. Hobbes exemplifies the philosophy of individualism that, as I say, lies at the base of the Anglo-American view of the world.

II
Holism

Hobbes sees the whole as made from the parts. One starts with the parts, namely individuals, and builds wholes, namely societies. The parts, the individuals, are real, natural; the whole, the commonwealth, is artificial and therefore fragile.

Holism would take the opposite view. The whole is real, grounded in nature. It is the parts that are artificial. In fact, they are rather recent constructions, differentiated from the whole to an extent, but still fundamentally embedded in it.

Three themes characterize holism. The first theme is collectivism. Emile Durkheim, the French sociologist and philosopher, took issue with the English philosophers, such as Hobbes and his descendants, who saw society as built from individuals, the whole assembled from parts. Durkheim argued that first came society, then the individual: first the whole, then the parts.

By "first" Durkheim was speaking both historically and ontologically. He meant that, in history, unless the group had existed, the individual—as a sensing, reasoning, willing creature, a human—could never have come to exist. He also meant that in our ongoing existence, now and forever, the group is more fundamental than the individual.

Durkheim's argument is speculative but suggestive. For example, he notes that thought patterns itself like society, for it proceeds by classification, by division into classes.[2] Society is constructed similarly. From such parallels, Durkheim argues that social experience is the basis for individual experience and thought. Of course, Durkheim is as relentless in arguing collectivism as was Hobbes in arguing individualism. As a student of Durkheim once said, the only way to escape Durkheim is to flee.

What might anthropologists say about this?

Anthropologists tend to do their research in societies that are rather collectivist. Classically, they studied so-called "primitives"—Malinowski's

---

[2]Emile Durkheim, *The Elementary Forms of the Religious Life* (New York: Collier, 1961).

Trobriand islanders,[3] Evans-Pritchards's Nuer,[4] Firth's Tikopia,[5]—small-scale societies that still exist in the remoter jungles, mountains, and islands, and comprise about 6 percent of the world's human population, though some 10,000 years ago they were 100 percent of it.

In these societies, the group—the community and clan—have a strength and power difficult for us to imagine. The dramatic instances are easiest to cite. In voodoo death, for example, if the group declares a person dead, he dies.[6] Conversely, in rituals of healing, if the group declares a person well, he gets well.[7] Here individual consciousness is so deeply enmeshed with group consciousness that it is not accurate to speak of individualism as we experience it. Now, these remarks oversimplify the character of the so-called "primitive" societies; individualistic, rationalistic, utilitarian values have their role in traditional societies too. Still, in broad comparison with our own lives, these statements hold.

More important than numbers is this point: the notion of individualism itself is a product of the group. The philosophy of individualism is, after all, a product of Western society. That unit we term "individual" is a construction that our culture has made, differentiating it as a part from the whole, abstracting it from the totality of human experience. Instead of Descartes's "I think, therefore I am," the Durkheimian collectivist would assert: "I *am*, I exist, as a product of my society and culture, therefore I *think*."

Individualism, whether Hobbesian or otherwise, sees the individual, the "I," the ego, as struggling against nature, whether his own—that is, his passions—or external nature, which in Tennyson's phrase is "red in tooth and claw." Gregory Bateson, British anthropologist and biologist, objects. In his *Steps to an Ecology of the Mind*[8] and his *Mind and Nature: A Necessary Unity*,[9] Bateson argues that it is fallacious to imagine the indi-

---

[3]*Bronislaw Malinowski, Argonauts of the Western Pacific* (London: G. Routledge, 1922).

[4]Edward Evans-Pritchard, *The Nuer* (Oxford: Clarendon, 1940).

[5]Raymond Firth, *We, the Tikopia* (London: Allen and Unwin, 1936).

[6]Walter B. Cannon, *The Wisdom of the Body* (New York: Norton, 1939).

[7]Victor W. Turner, *Drums of Affliction* (Oxford: Clarendon, 1968).

[8]Gregory Bateson, *Steps to an Ecology of the Mind* (New York: Ballantine, 1972).

[9]Gregory Bateson, *Mind and Nature: A Necessary Unity* (New York: Dutton, 1979).

vidual as separate from the environment. This fallacy is destroying both us and our environment.

The Western view of nature, rooted in Judeo-Christian theology, as restated by utilitarian philosophies of the Victorian age and since, sees the individual working *against* nature, fighting for a "survival of the fittest." Such a view lies behind exploitation rather than conservation of nature. Bateson objects because logically the organism that destroys its environment destroys itself. The unit of survival is not the *organism*; it is the organism *plus* its environment.

Bateson urges us to realize how the organism, or individual, and the environment are part of a single system. Western philosophers such as Descartes have so sharpened our sense of self that we assume our selves stop with our skin. For Bateson, if he is cutting down a tree, he, the axe, and the tree are all part of a single system. It would be arbitrary to draw a line where Bateson stops and the axe begins, or the axe stops and the tree begins. We need to transcend the lines we have drawn arbitrarily and grasp the interrelationships between ourselves and nature.

What might anthropology say about this? Anthropology would argue that humans can experience and assume a certain intimacy of relation between self and nature. In totemistic societies, for example, each group identifies with a natural category; there is the bear, the lion, and the wolf clan. The Bororo of Brazil are said to believe, in certain contexts, that they *are* the animal designated as their totem. In a sensitive writer such as William Faulkner, one sees a survival of such totemism in works such as "The Bear" or *As I Lay Dying*.

Having seen that human groups can and do experience a certain unity of self and nature, anthropology would be sympathetic, with qualifications, to Bateson's argument. He fits the wholistic emphasis. Just as an individual standing apart from society is an abstraction from the unity of experience, so is an individual standing apart from nature. Both abstractions have been accentuated by the development of the West and of the industrial and Protestant era. A more unified view is older in the human experience, and the truths of that view should be remembered.

At another level one may speak of the relation between man and his own nature. Hobbes saw this relation, too, as a battle. Reason fights passion; order is gained by control of our baser nature. Such a view has dominated Western psychology, though how control is to be achieved varies with the school of thought.

Freudian psychology, which has been more influential in America than anywhere else, seeks control of the passions, the id, the libido, by coming to know them. One renders the unconscious conscious through psychoanalysis.

British psychology of a type more directly akin to Hobbes apparently prefers not to know even the baser self. "Morbid introspection" was the British Victorian psychologists' view of looking within the human mind.[10] I note from perusing the telephone book that Oxford England lists only a fraction of the number of psychiatrists and psychologists found in Chapel Hill, North Carolina, even though Oxford is much larger. The British emphasis is on control of passions. Then there are the American psychologies of control, from Dale Carnegie to behavior modification.

Here we are tracing a particular, recent view of self in relation to our baser natures, the passions. This is a Western view, but one could find parallels in other historical civilizations established roughly at the same time as Christianity, notably Islam and Buddhism. Striking examples of psychologies of control in Chinese Buddhism could be cited, as in recent studies by Joseph Needham,[11] and Islam sees passions (*nafsu*) controlled by reason (*akal*) and ethics (*achlak*).[12]

Getting beyond these historic traditions and considering the full gamut of human experience, we discover that wholistic views are frequent. In this view, nature, whether our own or external nature, is seen as simply part of the totality of existence. Disease, healing, fears, and hopes, the unconscious and consciousness are seen more as a unity. We are rediscovering this, to a limited extent, in wholistic medicine and in pastoral theology, and much anthropological lore supports the wisdom of these trends, though they are still imprisoned by their cultural setting.

As you will notice, religion has already found its way into the discussion; and, of course, this is the message of wholism, that religion is inseparable from the rest of existence. But religion, as seen by anthropology, has a distinctive function. It provides meaning. By "meaning" is meant, in part, framing. As Robert Bellah put it, to frame, to locate an act or object—

---

[10]Clark, "Morbid Introspection: Views of Psychopathology in Victorian Britain," a lecture in the seminar on the history of medicine, Trinity College, Oxford University, spring 1981.

[11]Joseph Needham, "Chinese Alchemy," lecture, Oxford University, spring 1981.

[12]James Peacock, *Muslim Puritans* (Berkeley: University of California Press, 1978).

a slice of our lives—within some broader scheme is to render that act or object meaningful.[13]

If the Frenchman Durkheim was the philosopher of collectivism, the German Max Weber is the sociologist of meaning. Weber illustrated the process of bestowing meaning by his study of the Protestant ethic.[14] According to Weber, the Calvinist Puritans craved salvation and feared damnation, so they sought a way to assure themselves that they were of the elect, not the damned. Finally, they decided that if you "worked like the devil," you could claim to be of the elect, for work could be seen as serving God. In this way work came to take on religious meaning; Calvinist religion rendered work meaningful, in fact, sacred. As a by-product, heirs of the Protestant tradition feel guilty if they don't work.

As Weber realized, religion gives meaning to life in many respects. Religion must make sense out of a world in which rain falls on the just and the unjust, and the unjust flourish like the green bay tree. It must make sense out of suffering and despair, evil and death.

To this Weberian view, anthropology adds a footnote. Meaning is not merely thought. Religion is not simply theology or belief; it encompasses all experience. When the Australian aboriginal locates himself within his cosmos, which embraces his natural, desert environment, his animal and plant companions, his ancestral spirits, his rites, and his shrines, he is living meaning.

This aboriginal does not merely speculate about God or angel, creation or the afterlife; in a certain ritual, he falls into trance, and within it he begins to dream. As he dreams, he identifies with spirits—what I may call, after Joseph Conrad, "secret sharers." These secret sharers are spirits who are his ancestors but still alive. Thus the aboriginal comes to live, in the past as well as the future, in the eternal, what Stanner terms "everywhen."[15]

This sort of experience is what Rodney Needham implies when he demonstrates that the term "belief" is not suitable to describe much of religious

---

[13]Robert Bellah, "Notes toward the Systematic Study of Religion," appendix to *Beyond Belief* (New York: Harper, 1970).

[14]Max Weber, *The Protestant Ethic and the Spirit of Capitalism* (London: Allen and Unwin, 1976).

[15]W. E. H. Stanner, "The Dreaming" in W. A. Lessa and E. Z. Vogt, *Reader in Comparative Religion: An Anthropological Approach* (New York: Harper and Row, 1958).

experience.[16] Belief, in fact, best suits those peculiarly textual and theological traditions from which we stem. A belief is a proposition: I believe there is a God; I believe in heaven. The relation of humans to the spiritual is deeper and more complex than this. I once asked an Indonesian, "Do you believe (pertjaja) in spirits?" He replied, puzzled, "Are you asking, do I believe what spirits tell me when we talk?"

III
The Good Life

The anthropological perspective, as presented here, emphasizes wholism. Life is a whole and one should try to see the whole, then grasp the relation between the parts and the whole. In the wholistic anthropological perspective, nature, group, and meaning are a unity. Only against that unity can other categories abstracted from it, such as "individual," be understood.

At this point the argument gets tricky. What has been stated is a view of the way things "are"—that existence is a whole, and that our peculiar culture has abstracted and emphasized certain elements in that whole such as "individual." What if this "is" is converted to an "ought"? That is, even if it is accepted that life is wholistic, or that the majority of human cultures have seen life wholistically, does that mean our culture should view life that way? Should we strive to better recognize and reinforce the unity between nature, group, meaning, and person?

This is essentially the view promulgated by anthropologist Levi-Strauss in his debate with the philosopher Sartre.[17] According to Levi-Strauss, Sartre argues that "history," which suggests individualism among other things, is the distinctive achievement of humankind; we should therefore celebrate and accentuate it. Levi-Strauss retorts that "history" is a very recent invention, while what he terms "totemism" (which involves what we've called "holism") is the most basic human pattern. For this reason, Levi-Strauss believed, we should emphasize holism.

Levi-Strauss argues from man's nature, Sartre from his destiny. Which should we do? For now, let us turn to ourselves. Consider where America stands along the continuum between individualism and holism.

---

[16]Rodney Needham, *Belief, Language, and Experience* (Oxford: Blackwell, 1972).

[17]Claude Lévi-Strauss, *The Savage Mind* (Chicago: University of Chicago, 1966).

IV

America

America, perhaps to a greater extent than Hobbes's England, had its origins in a quest for meaning. America was, to use Perry Miller's phrase, an "errand into the wilderness."[18] The New England colonies stemmed from a religious missionary impulse. The South had more of a commercial background and was, according to Samuel Hill,[19] "unreligious" until the eighteenth century, but then it became the Bible Belt.

In both North and South, the end result was a striking strength of independent denominations, whether Baptist, Methodist, Presbyterian, or Congregationalist. Unlike in England and Europe, there was and is in America no state church.

In 1904 Max Weber visited Mt. Airy, North Carolina, to stay with his cousin, who had migrated there. Weber witnessed a man baptized in an icy river. He asked why in the world anybody would subject himself to that. The Mt. Airy people replied, "He's about to open a bank." The point was that the man wanted to show he was pious and honest.[20] This observation led Weber to his study of relations between religion and capitalism in America. More broadly, he was struck with the strength of the Protestant denominations in America.

Weber, and other observers of America like de Tocqueville, understood that the Protestant denominations, and some others too, sustained a powerful religious influence in America that was independent of the state. They considered this a great strength of America. The voluntary denominational congregations and associations provided varied and independent bases for creating and sustaining meaning.[21]

Consider here the theme of collectivism. The usual observation is that America has moved from individualism to bureaucracy. William Whyte

---

[18]Perry Miller, *Errand into the Wilderness* (Cambridge: Harvard University Press, 1956).

[19]Samuel S. Hill, *Southern Churches in Crisis* (New York: Holt, Rinehart, and Winston, 1967).

[20]Max Weber, *From Max Weber* (New York: Oxford University Press, 1946).

[21]Edward Tiryakian "Marx, No; Durkheim, No; Weber, Perhaps," *American Sociological Review* 81 (1975): 1-33.

talked about the emergence of the organization man,[22] who was depicted in fiction as "the man in the gray flannel suit." David Riesman spoke of shift from inner- to other-directed. Americans became, wrote Riesman, like the little pig, crying "we, we, we."[23]

Talcott Parsons, drawing on Weber, more astutely observes that America has never been strictly individualistic. Although American ends are individualistic (e.g., pursuit of happiness), the means are voluntary groups.[24] Among such groups, and notably so, are the denominational groups.

We may speak of big government in America, but compare us to Europe. There government is bigger and independent denominationally based institutions are smaller. Look at Wake Forest, or at the other private, denominational colleges in North Carolina alone—Baptist, Moravian, Methodist, Lutheran, Quaker. In Britain, Germany, or Sweden, one finds no Wake Forest, Salem, Duke, Lenoir Rhyne, or Guilford. Again, it is possible to see that the independent, private denominational groups are a distinctive strength in America. (A footnote. Remember the paradox noted by John Wesley. Wesley's words, intended for Methodists, were initially inspired by Puritan ideals of frugality and industry, but these necessarily produced riches. Riches in turn produced worldliness, hence a decline in the spiritual impulse that had initiated the process.[25])

Similarly, at a more secular level, the American-style ideology of individualism gave rise to the voluntary, private business organization. These too produced riches and culminated in the giant corporate structures which, private though they may be, are the seat of the organization man, hence threaten the individualism that initiated their growth.

These paradoxical processes are part of the experience of the great denominational organizations in America, as well as of the business organizations. They are the wheelbarrow smuggled through the gate.

Now to address the third theme, nature. Man over nature has long been a dominant theme in America. It is part of the heritage of conquering the wilderness, reinforced by a certain aspect of the Protestant ethic that urges victory over nature.

---

[22]William H. Whyte, *The Organization Man* (Garden City NY: Doubleday, 1956).

[23]David Riesman, *The Lonely Crowd* (New Haven: Yale, 1967).

[24]Parsons Talcott, lecture, Harvard University, spring 1962.

[25]Weber, *The Protestant Ethic*.

Henry Glassie, the folklorist, points out that the rough-hewn log cabins popular in American myth of the frontier were, in fact, myth. Really, says Glassie, the frontiersmen smoothed their logs to accentuate the distinction between themselves and raw nature.[26]

The individual-over-nature ideal then got projected into the vast American technology that bulldozed everything. The reaction is the ecological movement, which dreams of restoring a balance between nature and mankind.

Parallel to the theme of mankind conquering outer nature was that of mankind conquering inner nature. America doubtless boasts more self-help books and self-help psychologies than any country. I've already mentioned such distinctively American therapies as behavior modification. A few responses to this are holistic medicine, the Eastern-inspired meditation movements, and other psychologies that crave unity.

In the area of relating humanity to nature, the traditional Protestant groups have been less notable than the Catholics, who developed pastoral monasticism; perhaps one reason relates to the Puritan mistrust of nature, both outer and inner. On the other hand, the distant offspring of the sectarian tradition, the counterculture groups, the whole earth people, and of course the German sects, such as the Amish and Hutterites, have notably striven for unity of humanity and nature in agrarian communes. And one should not forget the Protestant value on stewardship of nature.

V
Whither?

We have considered a philosophical tradition, individualism, from which we stem. We have considered an anthropological perspective, holism. We have considered the present pattern of American life.

Where might we now go?

A sensible design would draw strength from all three patterns: individualism, which emphasizes developments distinctive in recent history; holism, which recognizes patterns pervasive in all human existence; and America, which is what we have, where we are.

What focus might distill these strengths into some concrete activity or organization? The denominational, private religious group is perhaps the distinctive element in American culture. Such a group can combine indi-

---

[26]Henry Glassie, lecture, University of North Carolina at Chapel Hill, spring 1977.

vidualism and holism. It affirms the individual—the voluntary, free, reasoning, and willing person—yet it affirms also that he is necessarily part of the group, and it grounds the person in meaning. It could, though it has often not sufficiently done this, reinforce harmony and intimacy between man and his nature, both inner and outer.

Such groups, however, stand in danger of extremism. The trouble with sectarian groups is that they can become *too* sectarian. Jonestown is a recent, tragic case in point, though I am not convinced that the media have given the Reverend Mr. Jones a fair shake. But all sectarian groups must ask themselves certain questions. They are these. Can we sustain our particular values while affirming the broader values of our history and our culture and of humankind? Can we recognize and fertilize the creativity of the great traditions in science, the arts, and philosophy, the eloquence and beauty of literature, music, and liturgy? Can we uphold the noble traditions of genteel manners and folk progmation? The courage of the hero and the wisdom of the saint? Can the sectarian group do all these things while being adequately united, committed, and free?

We began with the image of a gate. Let us end with another gate image, but one more profound. In contemplating and choosing cultural as well as religious futures, remember humbly the teaching of St. Matthew (RSV, 7:13): "For the gate is narrow, and the way is hard, that leads to life, and those who find it are few."

ANTHROPOLOGY AND THEOLOGY: CONFRONTATION OR DIALOGUE?

E. Pendleton Banks

When anthropologists and theologians meet they tend to circle each other warily. The anthropologist expects the theologian to be an advocate of a particular religion and even of a particular denomination or sect and thus a prisoner of a narrow set of premises, while the theologian suspects that the anthropologist is lost in a heresy of "secular humanism" or "scientism." Then, each being aware of the other's perception, the anthropologist is likely to respond by being aggressively iconoclastic and the theologian by being defensively dogmatic. Each may in the end accuse the other of having a closed mind and a limited view.

This scenario is not inevitable. It is true that there are fundamental differences in point of view between the anthropologist, schooled in the comparative study of cultures, and the theologian, who often is an ordained minister and typically a committed believer in a particular faith. The anthropologist to be true to his discipline must see Christianity as another case of a religious tradition embedded in a particular cultural matrix. Yet anthropology has a long tradition of cultural relativism; anthropologists are professionally trained to approach any cultural manifestation, however bizarre, with a kind of determined empathy. Nothing human is alien to them. If cannibalism and human sacrifice can be understood in their appropriate contexts, the Christian mysteries should present no problem. And many theologians have become sophisticated in the anthropological literature; they have read Frazer, Durkheim, Malinowski, not to mention Margaret Mead and Lévi-Strauss—or at least Eliade, Peter Berger, and Harvey Cox, who have read the anthropological literature for them.[1]

---

[1]For a convenient sampling of the anthropological literature on religion, see Lessa and Vogt 1972.

So there are possibilities for fruitful dialogue between the two groups. Even so, there are likely to be problems of communication. Two different vocabularies are used; sometimes the same word has different meanings in the two disciplines. "Anthropology" to a theologian may mean simply the metaphysical examination of the nature of human being rather than a complex discipline comprising physical anthropology, archaeology, and cultural anthropology. The theologian may expect anthropologists to be specialists in social problems and social reform; some are, but these subjects are more likely to be the preoccupation of sociologists. The theologian who does not know the difference between anthropology and sociology will soon be corrected.

Even where there is a residue of misunderstanding, both disciplines can profit from a critical examination by outsiders. Modern theology, in my opinion, has gained more than it has lost by widening its horizons and responding to the comparative perspective of anthropology, while anthropology was rejuvenated by the "meta-anthropological" critique of David Bidney.[2] Specific theories and conceptual approaches borrowed from the one discipline can enrich the other. A. F. C. Wallace's theory of revitalization movements, derived from the study of American Indian and other movements that occurred in response to the stress of foreign domination, has suggested new insights into the origins of Christianity.[3] Clifford Geertz, in turn, has been influenced by the hermeneutic approach of theology in his penetrating analyses of meaning in Indonesian and Moroccan cultures.[4]

I propose to comment on the papers in this volume in terms of their contribution to the dialogue and to examine some of the themes that recur in them. The authors were invited to address the topic of "the images of man, nature, and the supernatural in selected traditions and cultures." Some took the assignment more literally than others, but all attempted to illuminate some aspect of the topic. Three of the authors deal with the topic in three specific cultural contexts—Islam (Spencer), Buddhism (Spiro), and the Judeo-Christian tradition (Angell). One author (Runyon) defends the scientific approach to knowledge in the context of Christian theology, while another (Farley) advances a claim for the superiority of the Christian inter-

---

[2]Bidney 1953.

[3]Wallace 1956.

[4]Geertz 1960 and 1968.

pretation of the nature of human being. Another author (Cox) sees signs of the future of Christianity in the "postmodern" age in such movements as liberation theology and television evangelism. Another (Peacock) attempts to integrate the vision of anthropology with that of Christianity. Since the papers were written independently, no author attempts to debate particular issues with another, and some questions discussed by one author are not mentioned by others.

Yet inevitably the topical framework guarantees that some issues run through several of the papers. Further, the fact that three of the major traditions examined—Judaism, Christianity and Islam—have a historic connection while Buddhism comes from a cultural stream not completely independent predetermines a certain similarity in world view. An examination of tribal religions located outside the Old World *Oikoumene* would have yielded more heterogeneity.

I
Man

The nature of man is one of the perennial problems addressed by every religion and every culture. In Islam, as in Judaism and Christianity, man is defined as a creature of God, but there seems to be little interest in the metaphysics of human being as such. The believer is identified by his obedience to the will of God and by his visible observance of the "pillars of the faith": testimony, prayer, alms, fasting, and pilgrimage. The emphasis on '*ummah*, the community of believers, suggests that the nature of the individual person can only be defined with reference to the social group. Indeed, in Spencer's view the most distinctive aspect of Islam is the social order it created; the conflicts between that order and the modern world continue to generate many of our daily headlines. Judaism, like Islam, sees man as a part of nature, but introduces the concept of spirit and therefore of transcendence. The idea of a community of believers is related to the concept of covenant, which is a relationship both among men and between God and man. Christianity builds upon Jewish foundations but with different emphases: otherworldliness, mysticism, and dualism enter the picture. Sin and redemption become essential components of the human condition. Perhaps surprisingly, Christianity becomes as thoroughly universalistic as Islam.

The Buddhist theory of human being breaks sharply with the other traditions. Not only is all that we take to be sensate reality revealed as illusion, so is the existence of the individual human being. *Anatta*, the negation of self, is a basic premise. Yet, as Spiro demonstrates, in the popular practice of Theravāda Buddhism in Burma this premise is ignored and the continuity of the individual soul through rebirth is assumed. Once that step has been taken, Buddhism does not seem to require any particular theory of human nature. Depravity can be overcome by works of merit or by meditation; if human nature is essentially good, the process of salvation is merely facilitated.[5]

II
Nature

The most important thing about various theories of nature is not so much what they say nature *is* as how the relationship between man and nature is conceived. All of the traditions under consideration see nature as God's creation (though Buddhism sometimes seems to beg the question) and therefore man is placed from the beginning in some kind of special relationship with nature. Genesis lays the groundwork for the Judeo-Christian position that nature is for man's use. Lynn White has argued that modern environmental problems can be traced to this exploitive attitude toward nature.[6] The counterargument that people of other traditions also have degraded their environments does not by itself refute White's thesis, since different causes may produce the same effect; however, some environmentalists find a basis for their attempts to restore and conserve nature in the Christian concept of stewardship. Spencer rightly emphasizes the earthy practicality of Islam in its approach to material things, including money. Christianity, with its tendencies to mysticism and spirituality, sometimes seems to occupy the other end of the continuum, with Judaism somewhere in the middle; yet modern science and technology are the historic descendants of Christianity, and the obsessive materialism of both capitalism and socialism follows from the Protestant Reformation.[7]

Again Buddhism, by denying the existence of the natural world, defines a distinctive relationship; the devout Buddhist seeks salvation through a profound detachment. On the other hand, Burmese Buddhists find an ac-

---

[5]The question of free will is not addressed here; it deserves a more comprehensive treatment than space permits. One has the impression that of the major religious traditions, only Christianity tackles the question directly in all of its complexity and paradox.

[6]White 1967.

[7]Weber 1930.

commodation with nature and express their faith by showing a reverence for at least the higher forms of animal life. (It is puzzling that Islam, Judaism, and Buddhism, starting from different premises, arrive at strict food taboos, while Christianity, though sharing many premises with Islam and Judaism, has been relatively free from such preoccupations.)

III
The Supernatural

An anthropologist from another planet would find great similarities in the Islamic, Jewish, and Christian theories of the supernatural. They clearly derive from the same historic tradition of monotheism (though a closer look would show a strain of dualistic thinking in Christianity). After a few years spent reading modern Christian theology, however, he might conclude that almost any point of view imaginable could be found in Christianity alone. He might in the end find that Christian thought diverges from both Judaism and Islam in emphasizing a special, personal relationship between God and the individual. In any case Buddhism would be found occupying an isolated position, denying the existence of the supernatural along with nature and the individual soul. He would also note the failure of Burmese Buddhists to take this premise literally.

If he looked farther afield at the many tribal religions found on earth, he would find a greater variety of beliefs about the supernatural than about man or nature. (He might be forgiven for suspecting that a paucity of empirical data tends to make theology a field for the free play of human imagination.) Tribal cultures enrich the world with spirits, demons, and gods in infinite variety and provide themselves with colorful and complex rituals of propitiation and worship. Our interplanetary anthropologist might wonder in passing at the impoverishment of life that accompanies monotheism (although we could point to exceptions ranging from the cult of the saints in Christianity to the festivals of popular Buddhism).

Perhaps the clearest and most consistent view of the supernatural is found in Islam. God, in addition to being unitary, is eternal, omniscient, omnipotent, and compassionate. Further, God alone *is*, nothing else has any independent existence, and all that man needs to know about God is set forth in the Qurān. There is little room here for anthropological analysis or, one would think, for theological disputation.

All of the monotheistic religions agree on one thing: the proper attitude of man toward God is submission, worship, obedience. The only task left for the exercise of human intelligence is to find the proper forms of worship and to explore the implications of "obedience" for everyday behavior, as well as for social and political action.

IV
Culture

One issue not explicitly included in the topical framework for this group of papers emerges nonetheless in reading them: the relationship between religion and the rest of culture. Spencer focuses on the actualization of Islamic belief in historic and modern Islamic social, political, and economic institutions. Spiro finds his principal thesis in the contradictions between formal Buddhist doctrine and the popular culture of Burma. The other authors in a variety of ways direct our attention to the connections between faith and social reality (even when challenging prevailing ways of conceptualizing them, as Farley does).

Without attempting to rephrase the expositions found in the papers, we may observe that it is precisely on this issue that anthropology has much to offer. Since Boas and Kroeber laid down the agenda of the discipline in the early part of the century, anthropology has found its mission to be the reasoned analysis of culture, defined as the totality of learned patterns of behavior shared by the members of a society. While this perspective may offend believers and theologians by making religion one of many categories of culture—along with language, art, social structure, technology, etc.—it has this advantage as a heuristic procedure: it focuses our attention on the interconnectedness, the integration (actual or potential) of cultural patterns. Since historically religions have never existed in a vacuum but always in a specific cultural context, a mode of thought that provides tools for the study of the context has an obvious value.

From this point of view, the key problem for religion in the contemporary world lies in the devastating impact of modernization—industrialization, mass communications, superstates, nuclear confrontation—on human life. The distinguished British anthropologist Sir Edmund Leach has given us the label "runaway world" for this phenomenon.[8] Each religion will seek its own answer to the runaway world—in the obscurantism of Khomeini's Iran or of some Christian Fundamentalists, the escapism of the monastic Buddhists, the "liberation theology" of the Catholic activists in Latin

---

[8]Leach 1968.

America. All too often the situation is made worse by conflicts between religious traditions. Surely it is not irrelevant to *our* search to try to understand what is happening. The dialogue between anthropology and theology (and not only Christian theology, at that) can contribute to our understanding.

Our problems are not going to be solved, in my view, either by a single religious tradition, uninformed by critical thinking and rational knowledge, or by a single academic school of thought, isolated from personal involvement. To solve them we need theologians (and believers) who can approach alien traditions with empathy and a hunger for understanding, and we need anthropologists (and other scholars and scientists) who will take religion seriously as a field of human thought and action.[9] We do not need "Christian" anthropology or "anthropological" Christianity so much as a continuing and lively dialogue between disciplines, carried on with mutual respect and goodwill. We hope that this volume will serve to indicate some of the directions the dialogue may take.

---

[9]Harvey Cox's willingness to do field work in Mexico City and in Lynchburg, Virginia, surely improved his understanding of contemporary trends in Christianity.

REFERENCES

Bidney, D.

1953　*Theoretical Anthropology.* New York: Columbia University Press.

Geertz, C.

1960　*The Religion of Java.* New York: The Free Press.

1968　*Islam Observed: Religious Development in Morocco and Indonesia.* New Haven: Yale University Press.

Leach, E.

1968　*A Runaway World?* New York: Oxford University Press.

Lessa, W. A. and E. Vogt

1972　*Reader in Comparative Religion: An Anthropological Approach.* New York: Harper and Row.

Wallace, A. F. C.

1956　"Revitalization Movements." *American Anthropologist* 58:264-81.

Weber, M.

1930　*The Protestant Ethic and the Spirit of Capitalism.* Translated by Talcott Parsons. London: George Allen and Unwin, Ltd.

White, L.

1967　"The Historic Roots of Our Ecological Crisis." *Science* 155:1203-1207.

THE CONTRIBUTORS

Angell, J. William, is Professor of Religion, Wake Forest University, Winston-Salem, North Carolina.

Banks, E. Pendleton, is Professor of Anthropology, Wake Forest University, Winston-Salem, North Carolina.

Cox, G. Harvey, is Professor of Theology, The Divinity School, Harvard University, Cambridge, Massachusetts.

Farley, Edward, is Professor of Theology, The Divinity School, Vanderbilt University, Nashville, Tennessee.

Peacock, James L., is Professor of Anthropology, University of North Carolina at Chapel Hill, North Carolina.

Runyon, Theodore H., Jr., is Professor of Theology, Candler School of Theology, Emory University, Atlanta, Georgia.

Spencer, Robert F., is Professor of Anthropology, University of Minnesota, Minneapolis, Minnesota.

Spiro, Melford E., is Professor of Anthropology, University of California at San Diego, La Jolla, California.

Index